BORED BOOMERS
ADULT COLORING BOOK

We confine your **masterpieces** to right-hand side pages only so you can cut them out and display them after coloring

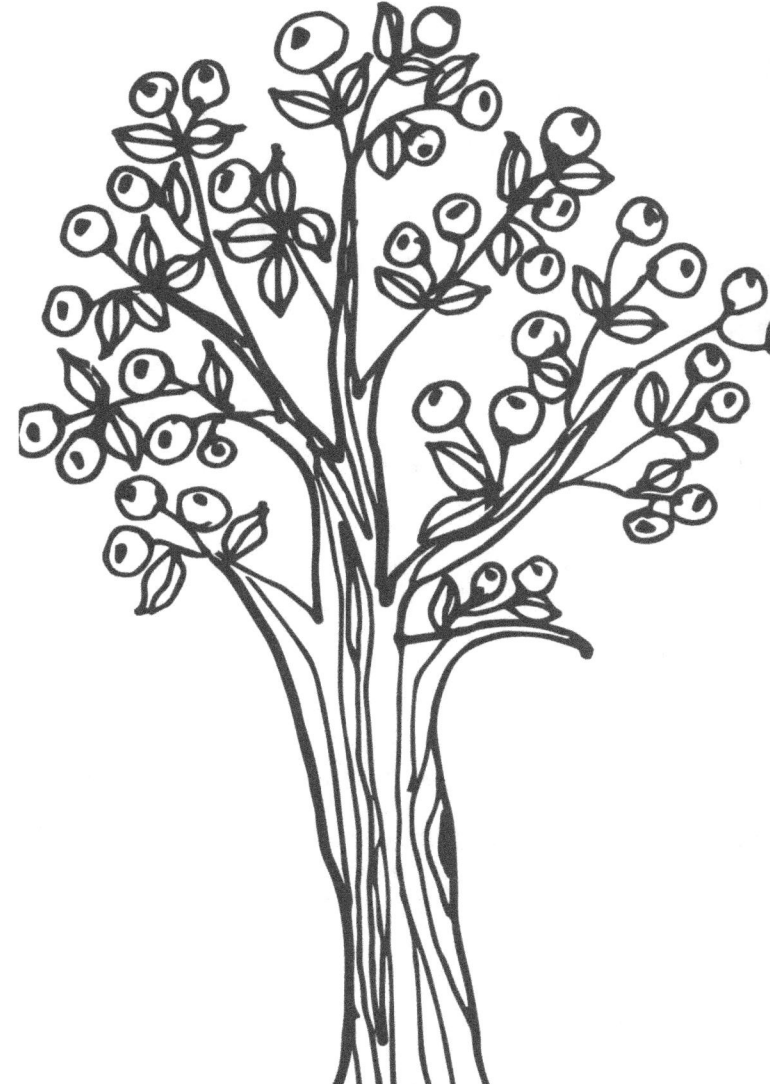

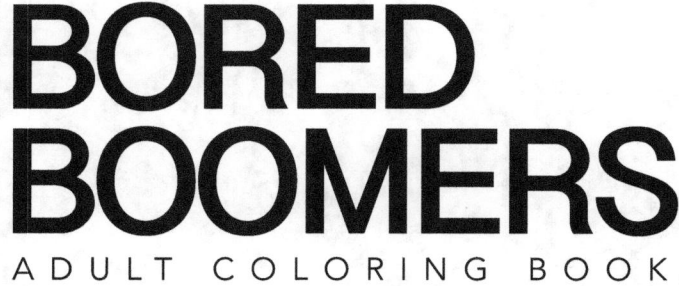
BORED BOOMERS
ADULT COLORING BOOK

ISBN: 9781670081957

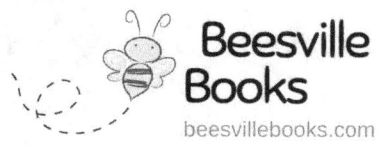

Copyright © 2019 Beesville Books
All Rights Reserved

The artwork used in this book is fully licensed to us by professional artists. This book contains material protected under International and Federal Copyright Laws and Treaties. Any unauthorized reprint or use of this material is prohibited. No part of the book may be reproduced or transmitted in any form or by any means, electronic or mechanical, including photocopying, recording, or by an information storage and retrieval system without express written permission from the author.

tester squares

Test your pencils and crayons here. Check for pencil hardness (and softness) and color saturation.

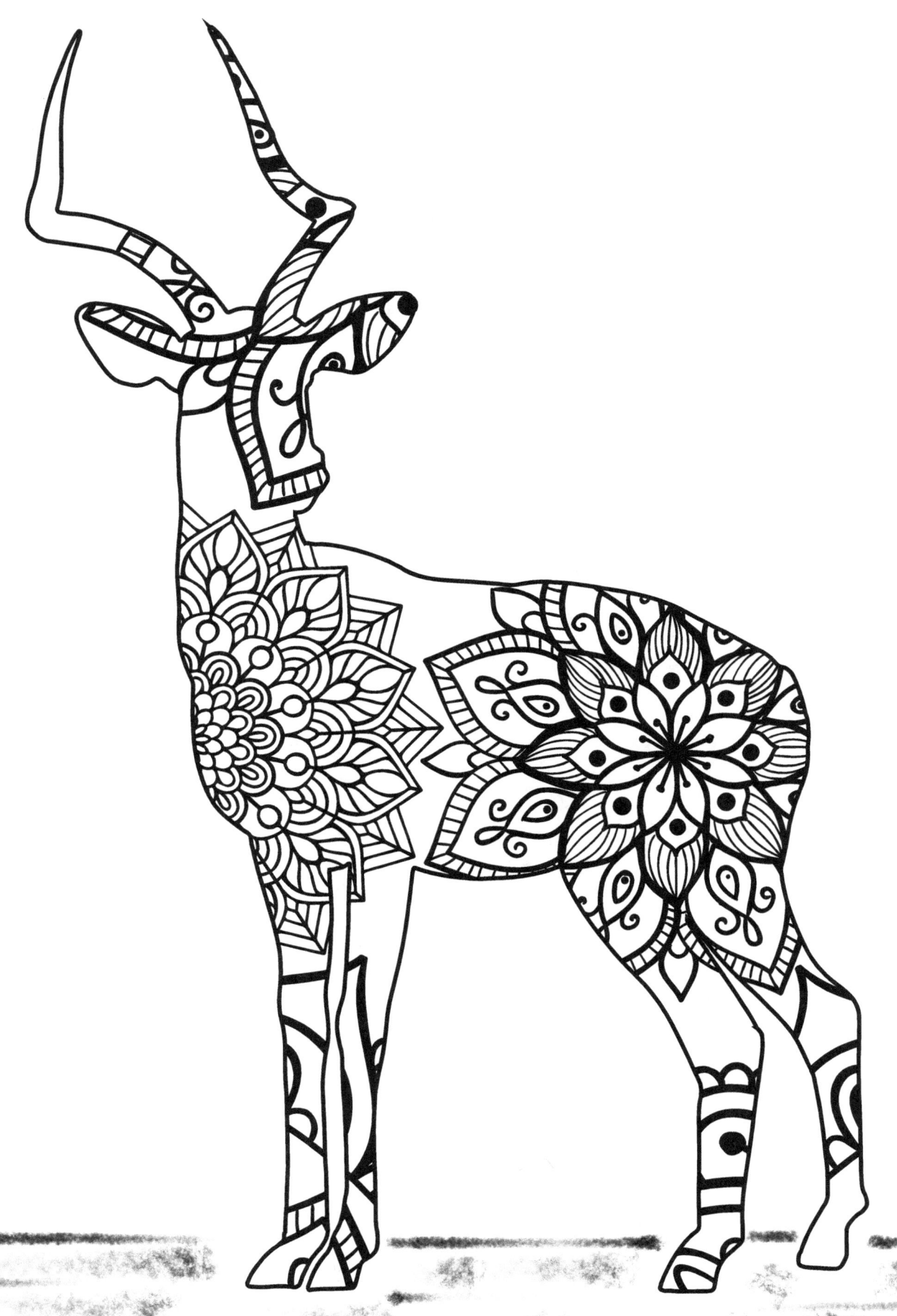

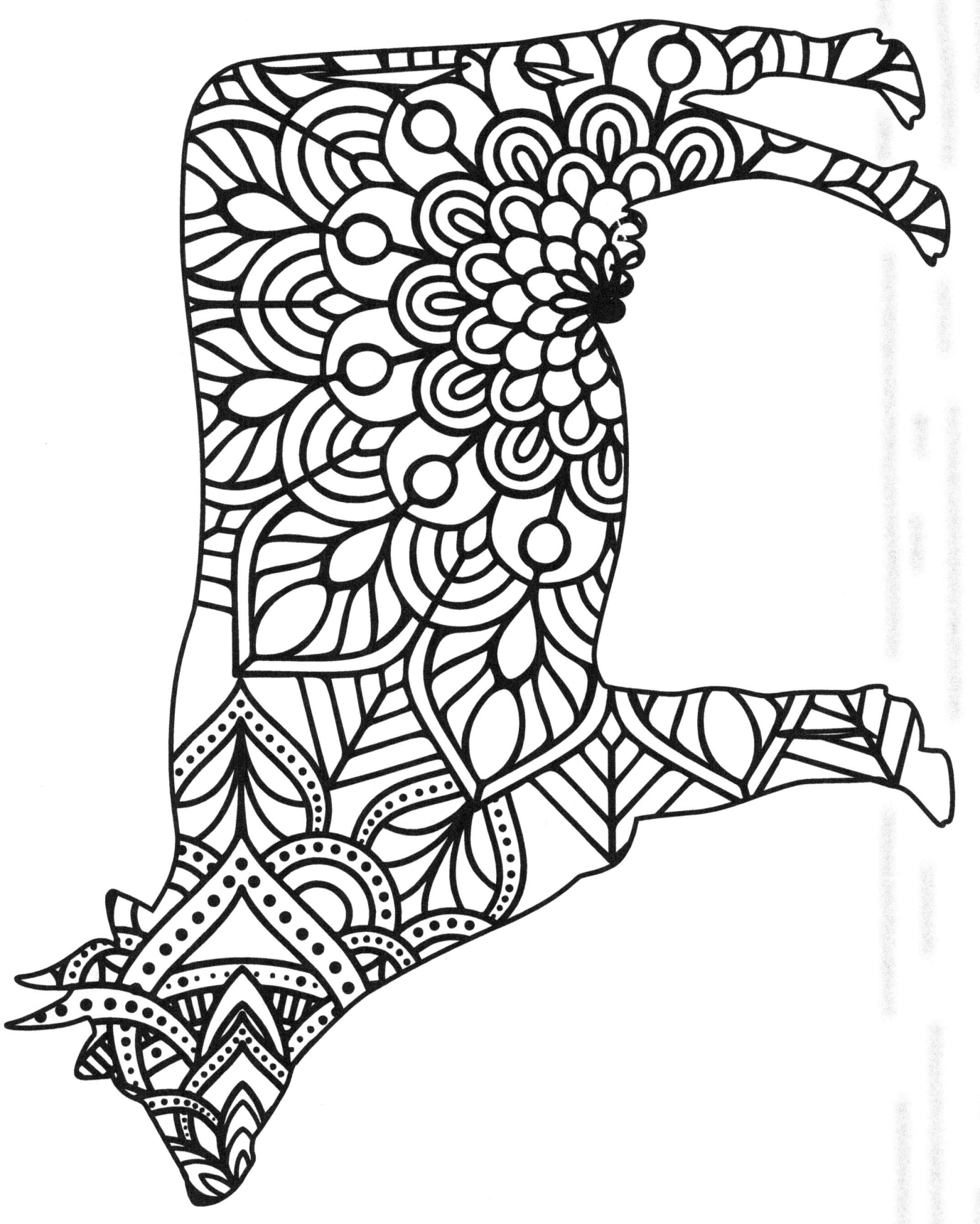

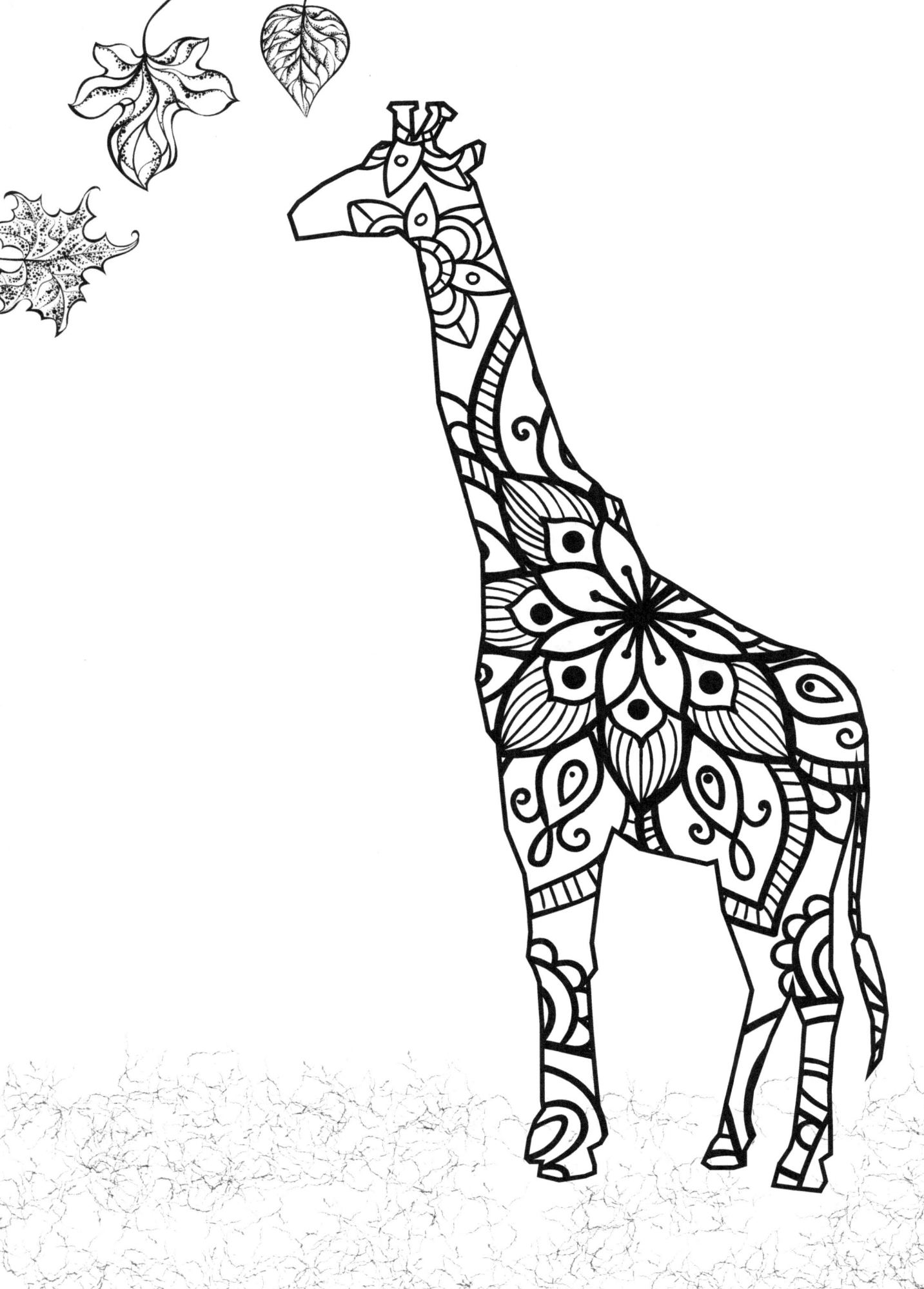

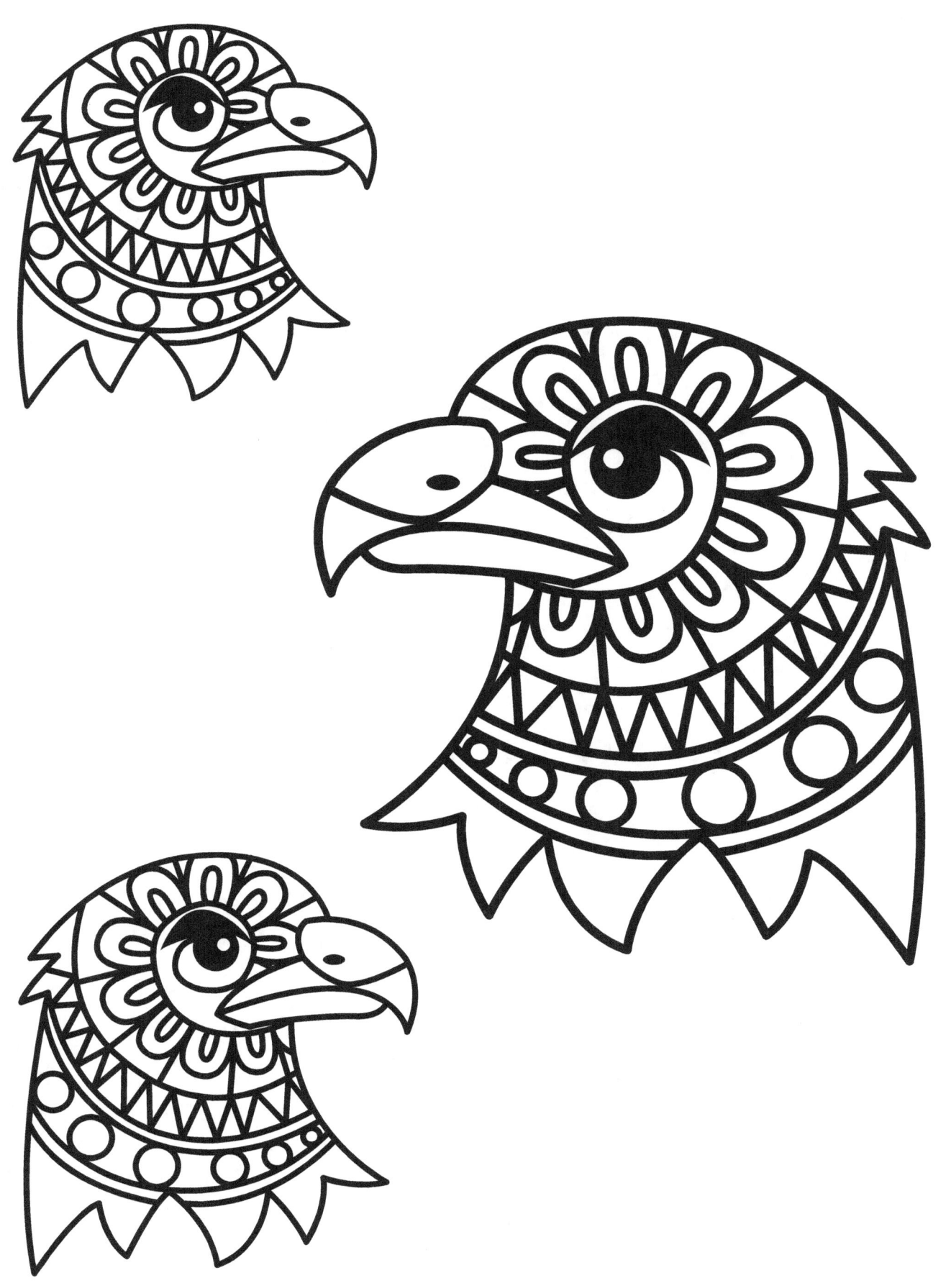

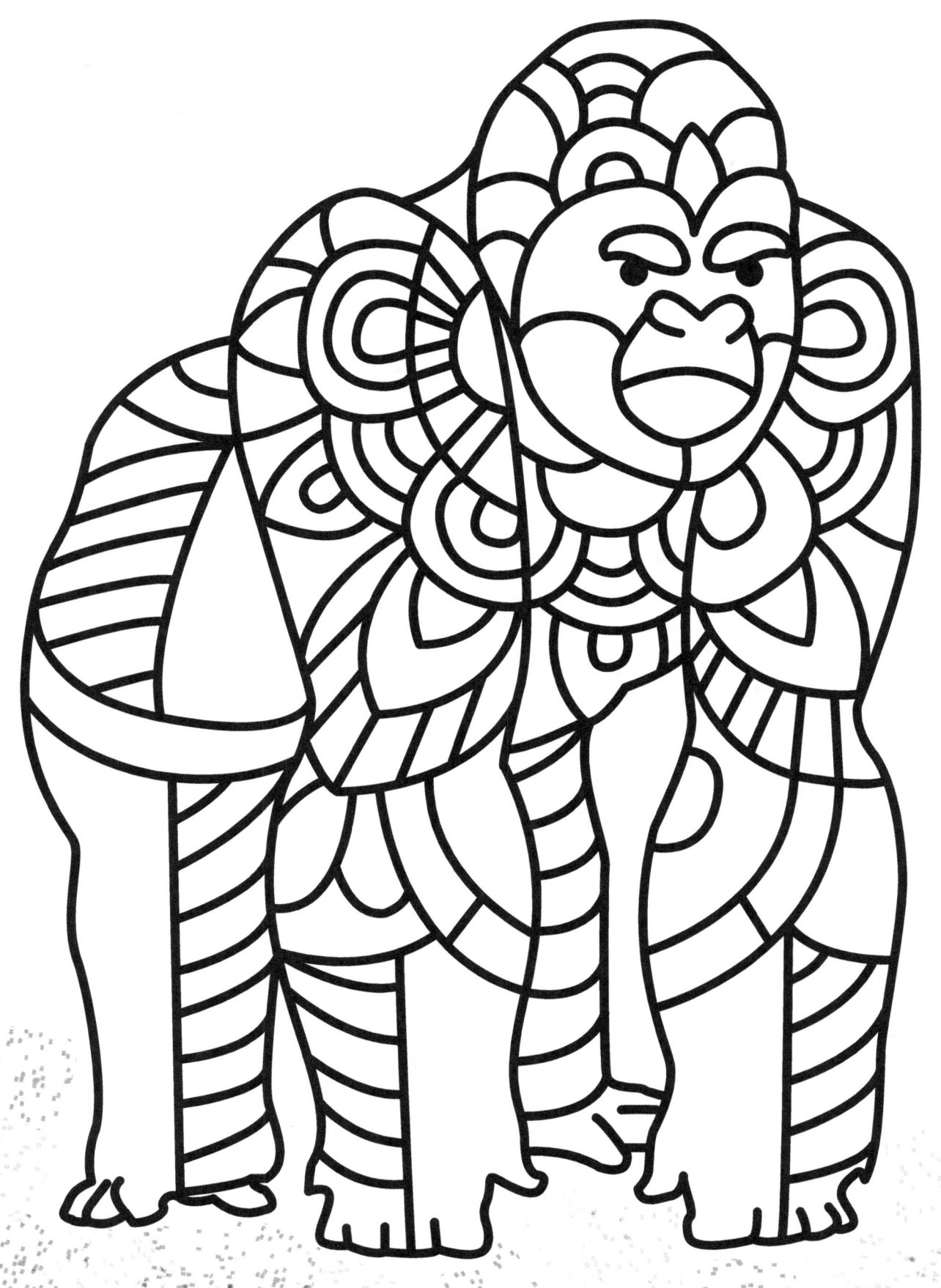

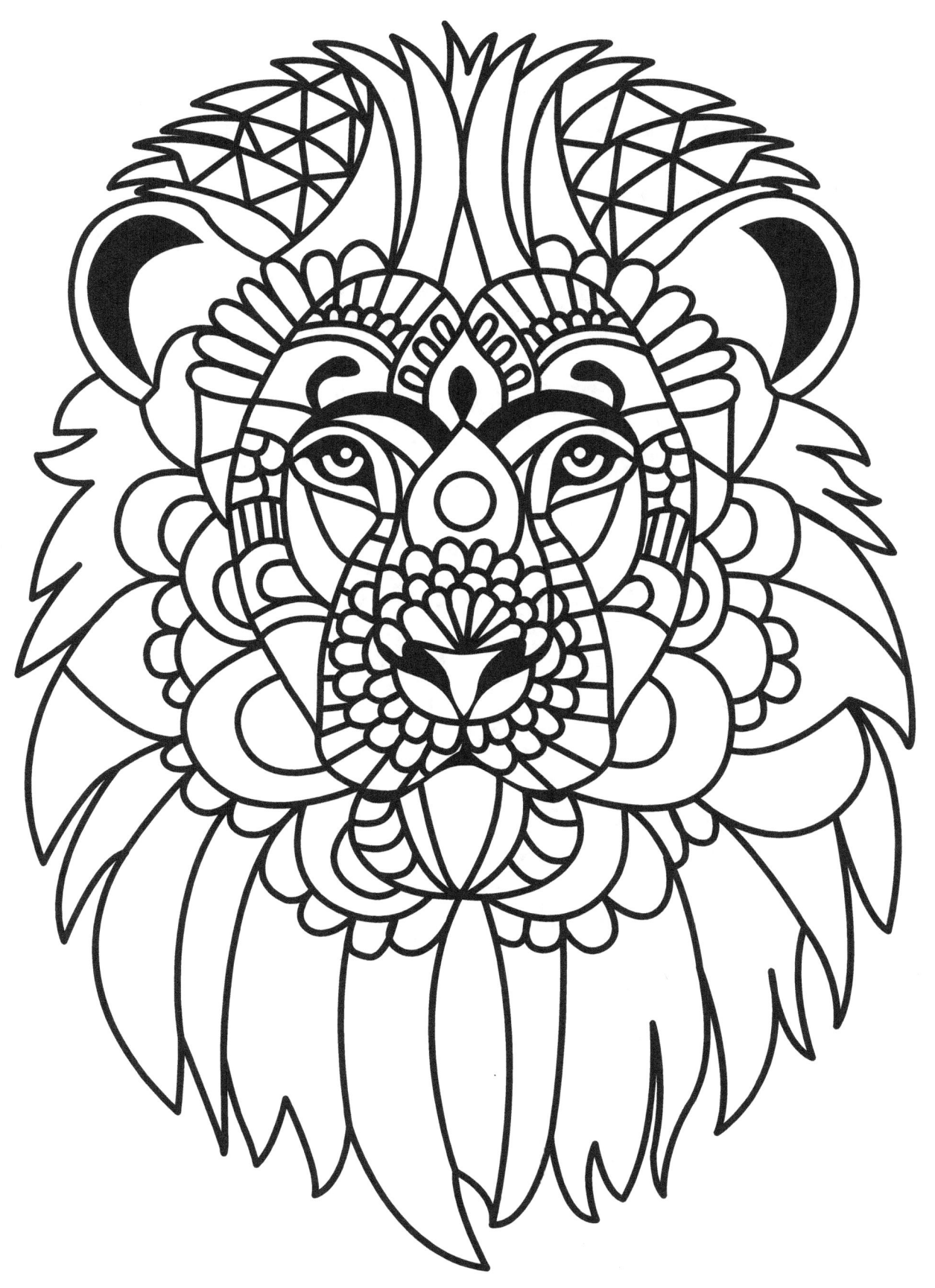

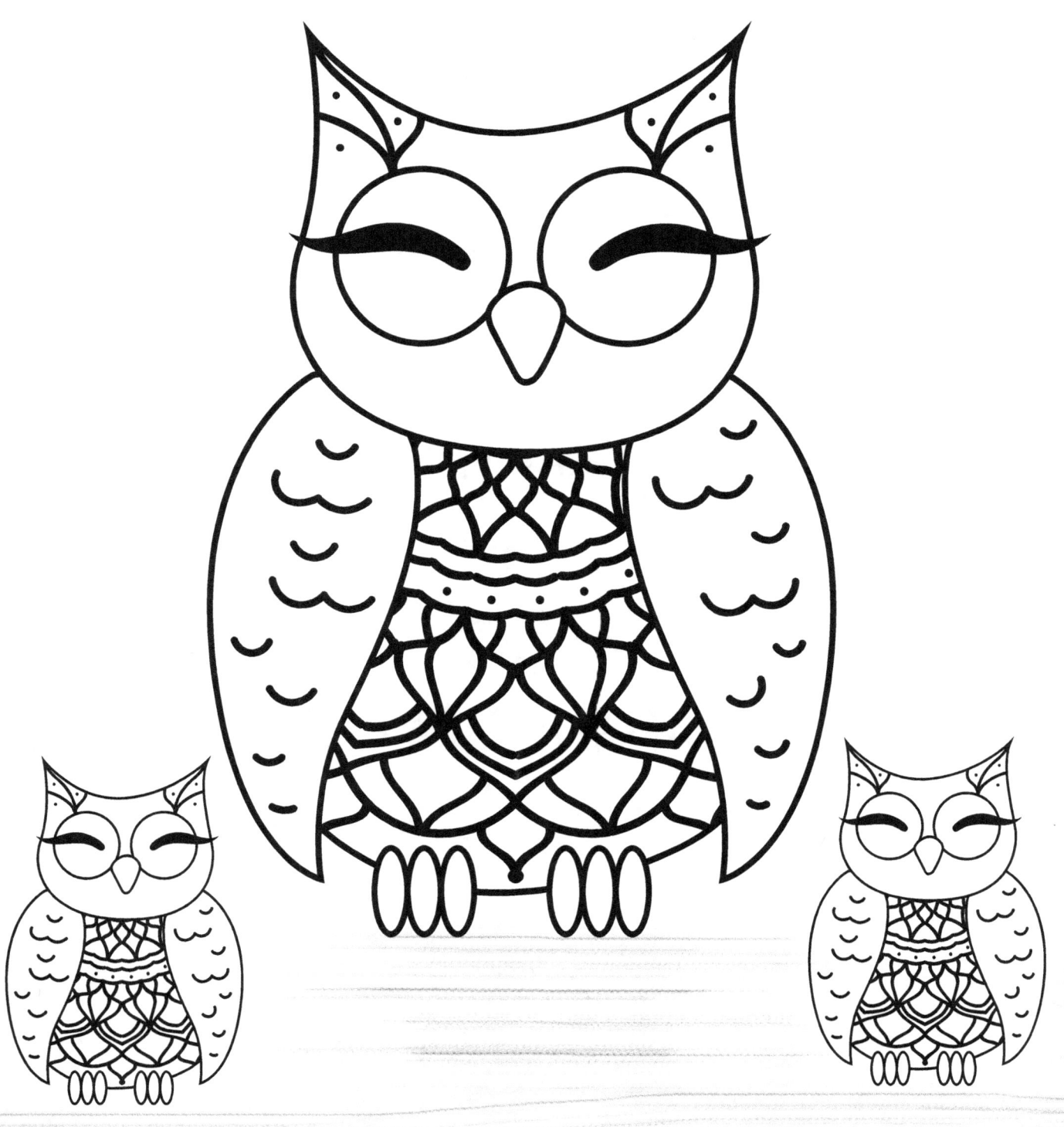

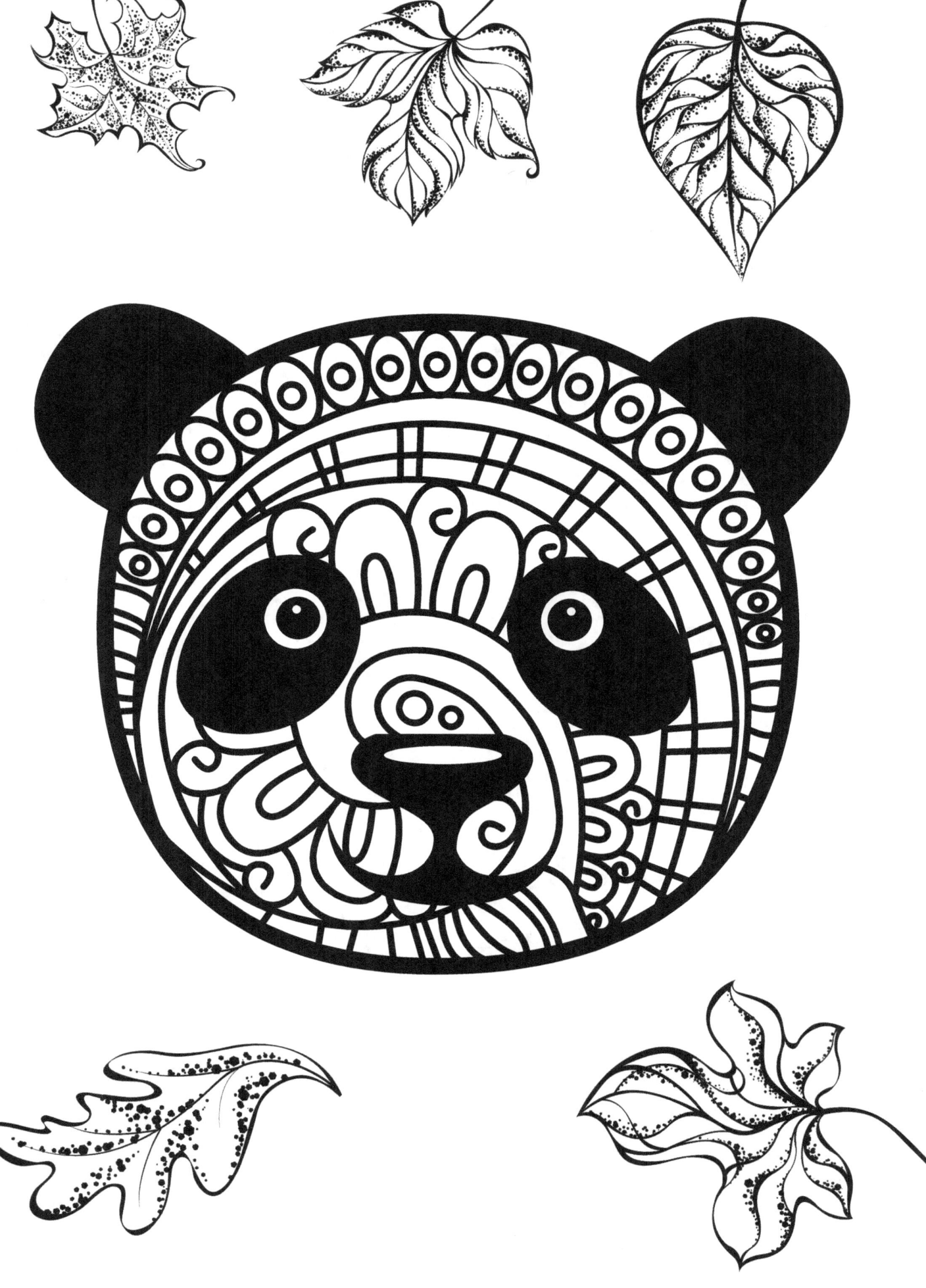

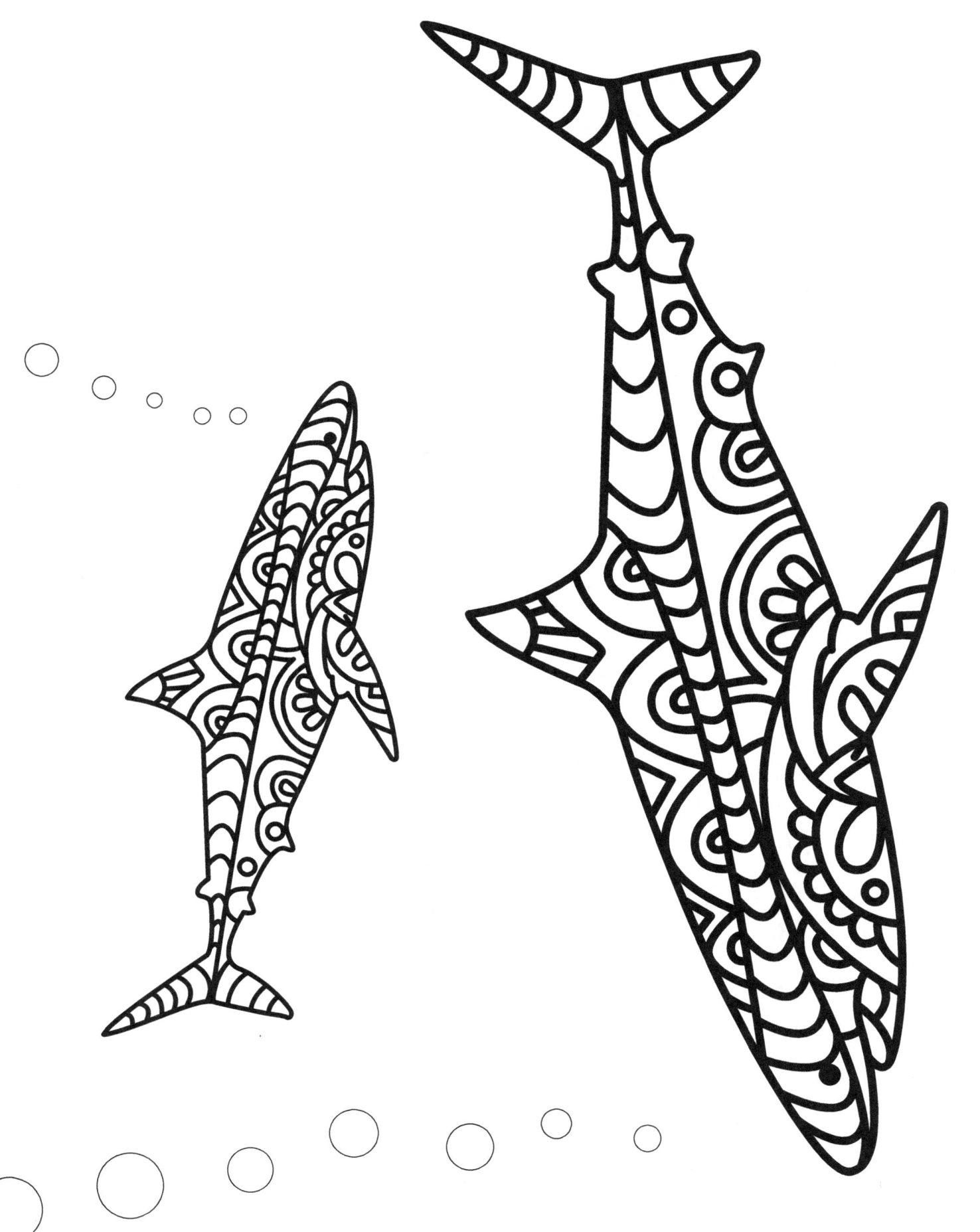

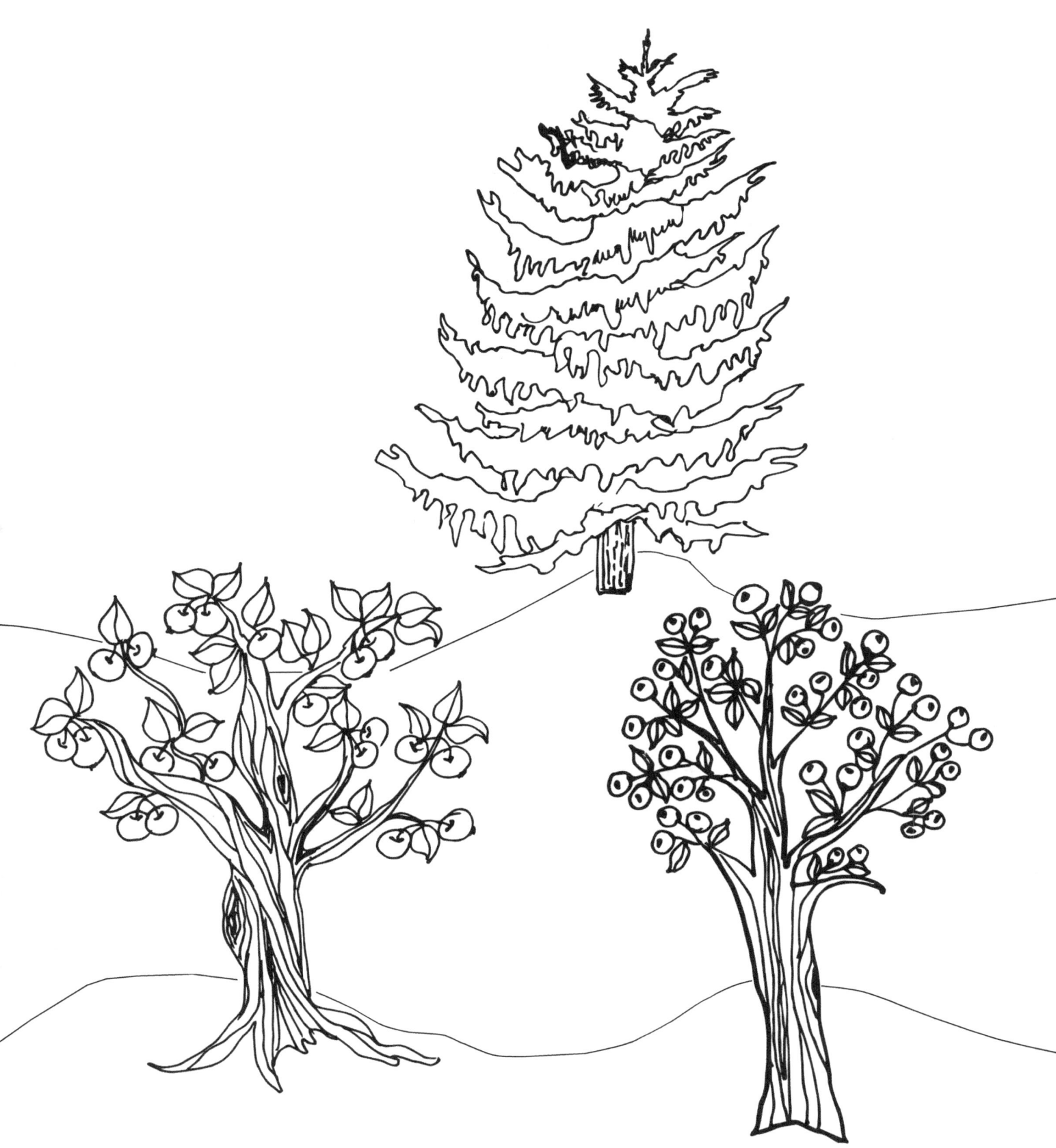

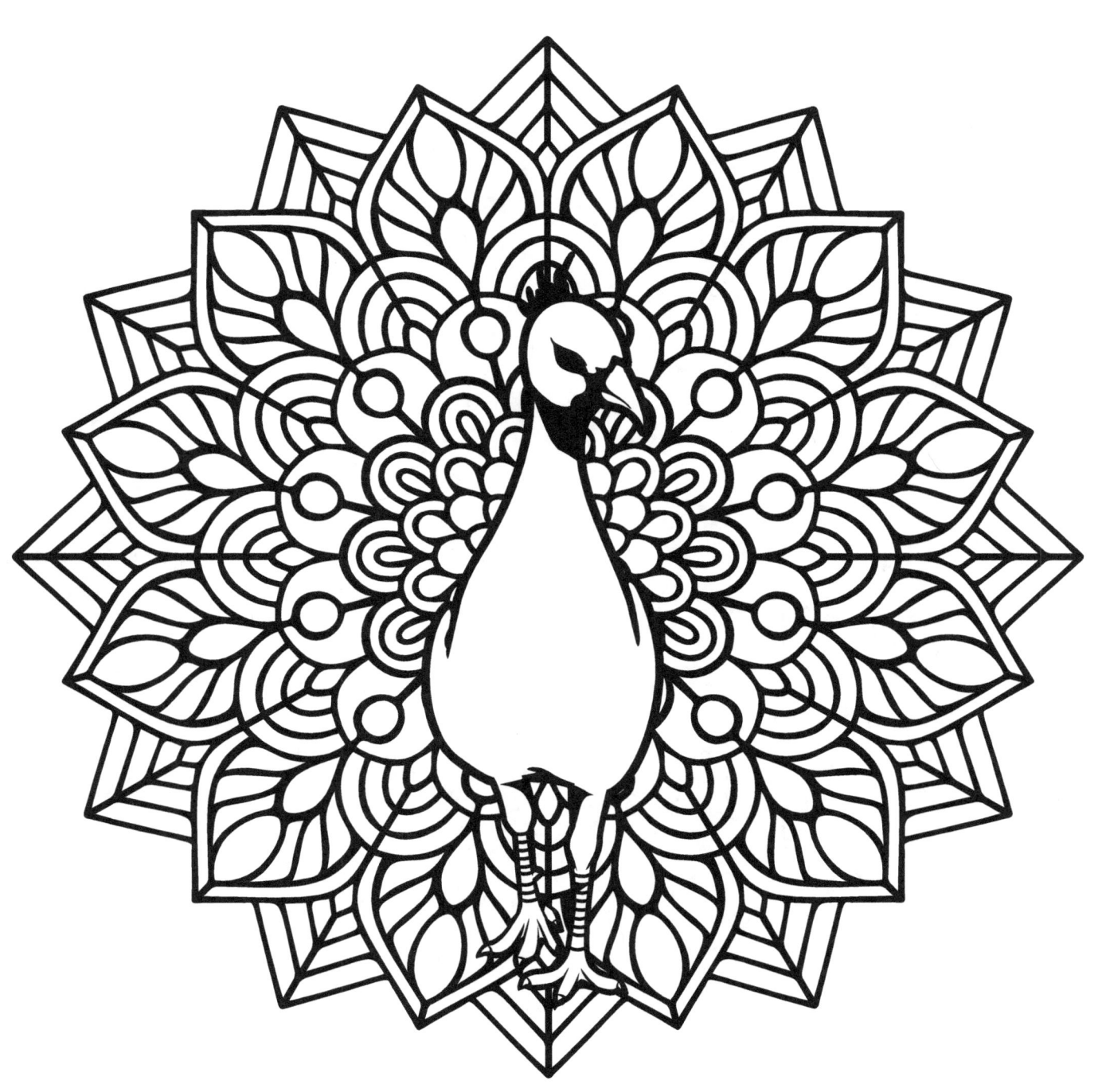

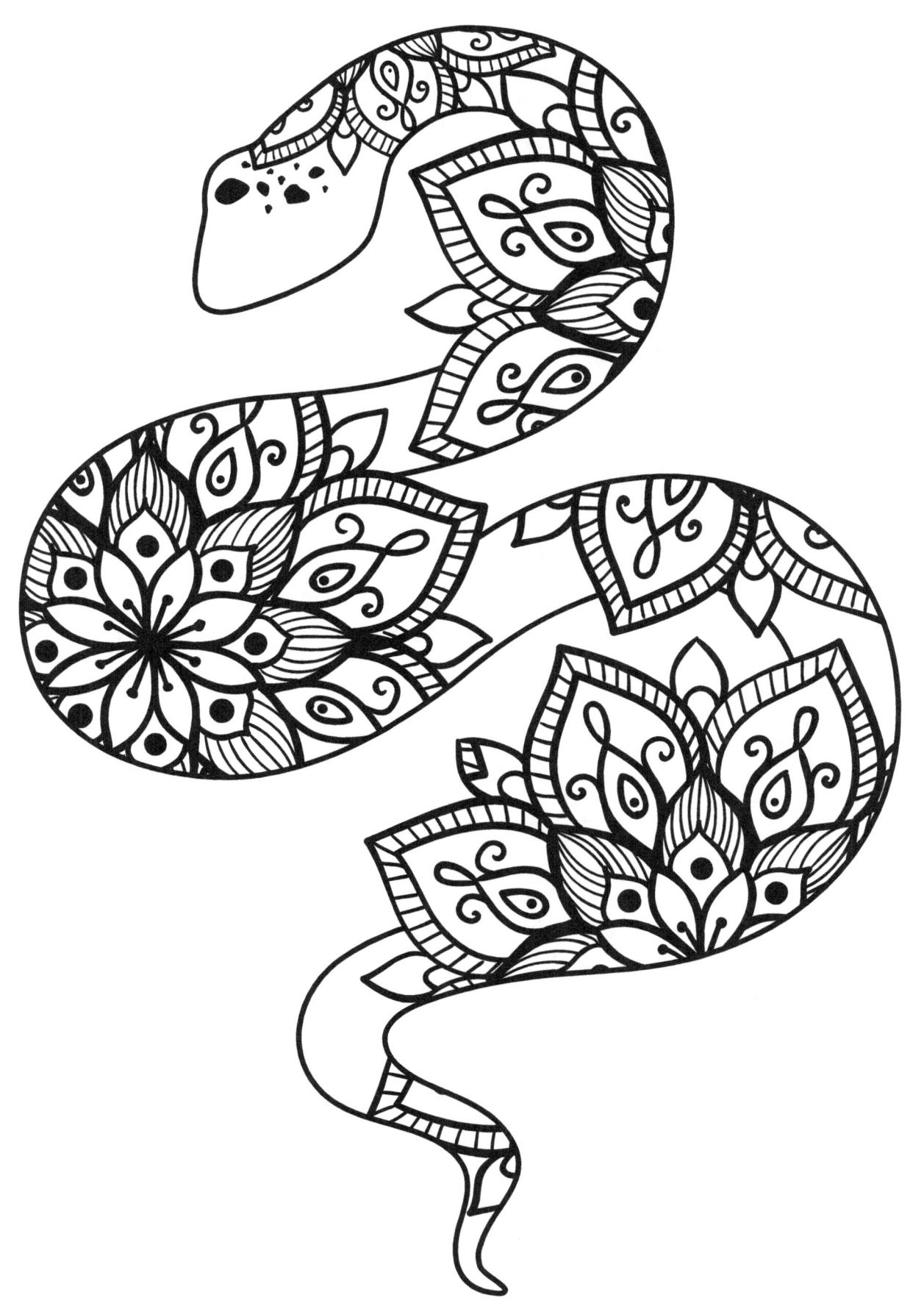

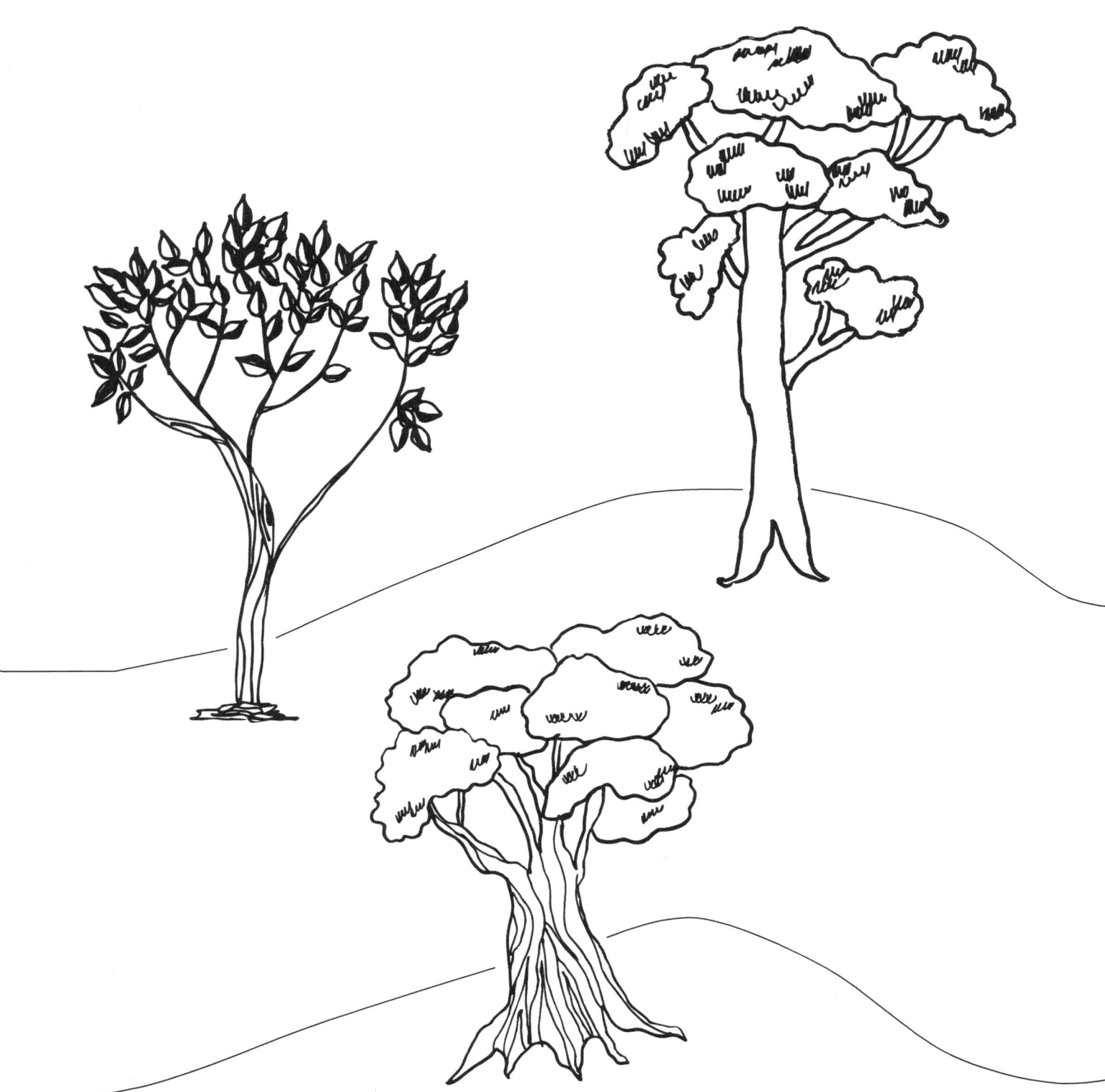

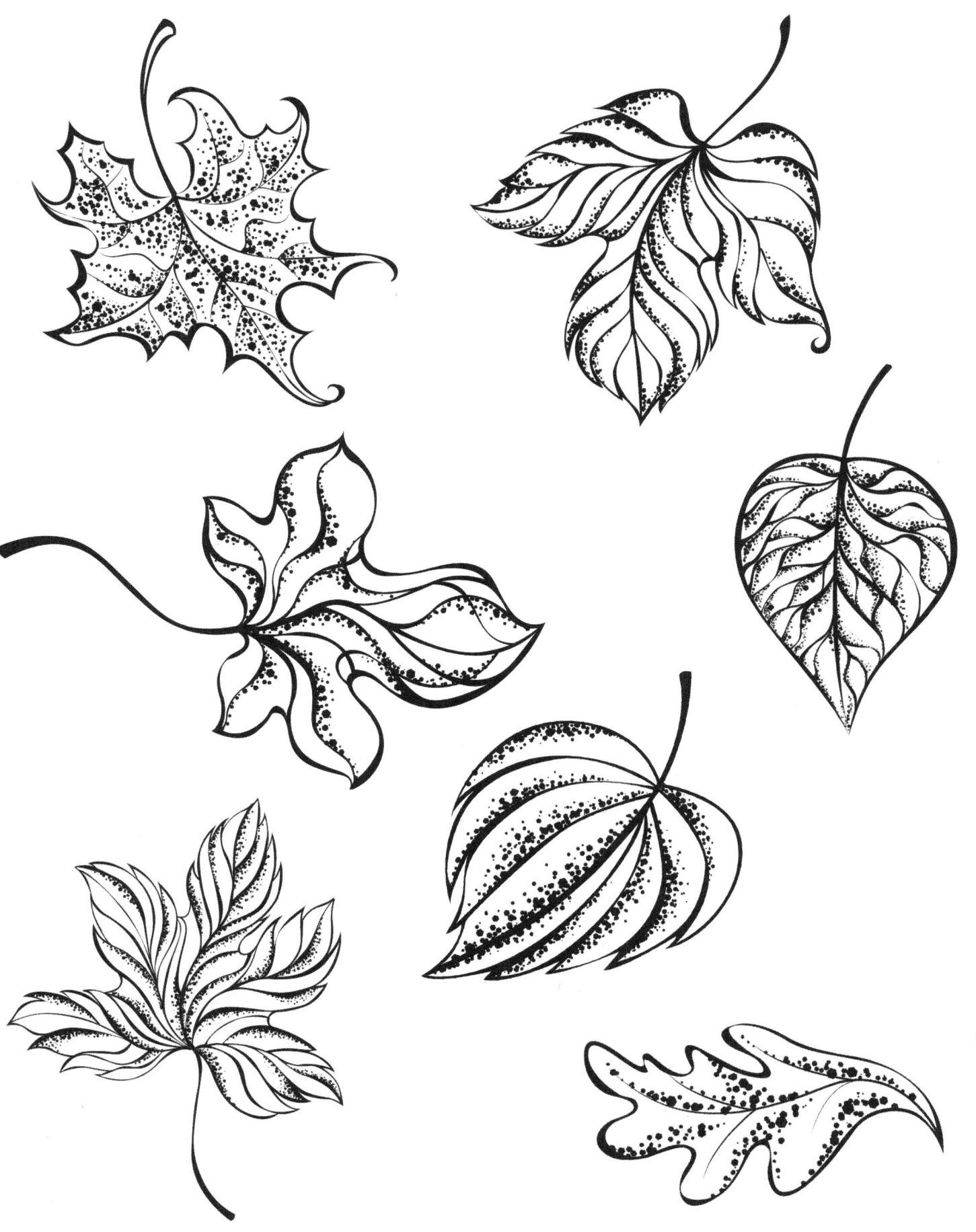

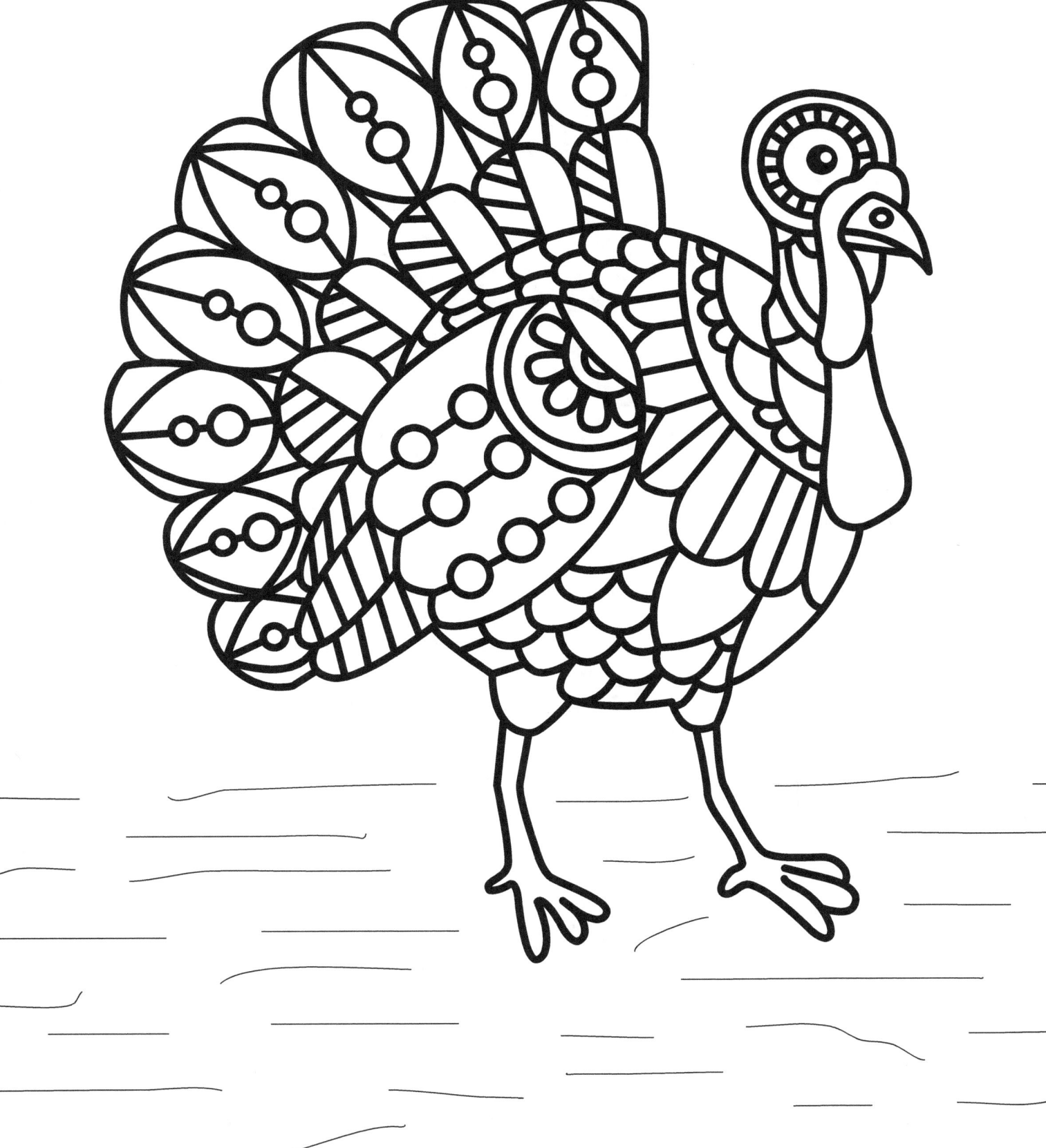

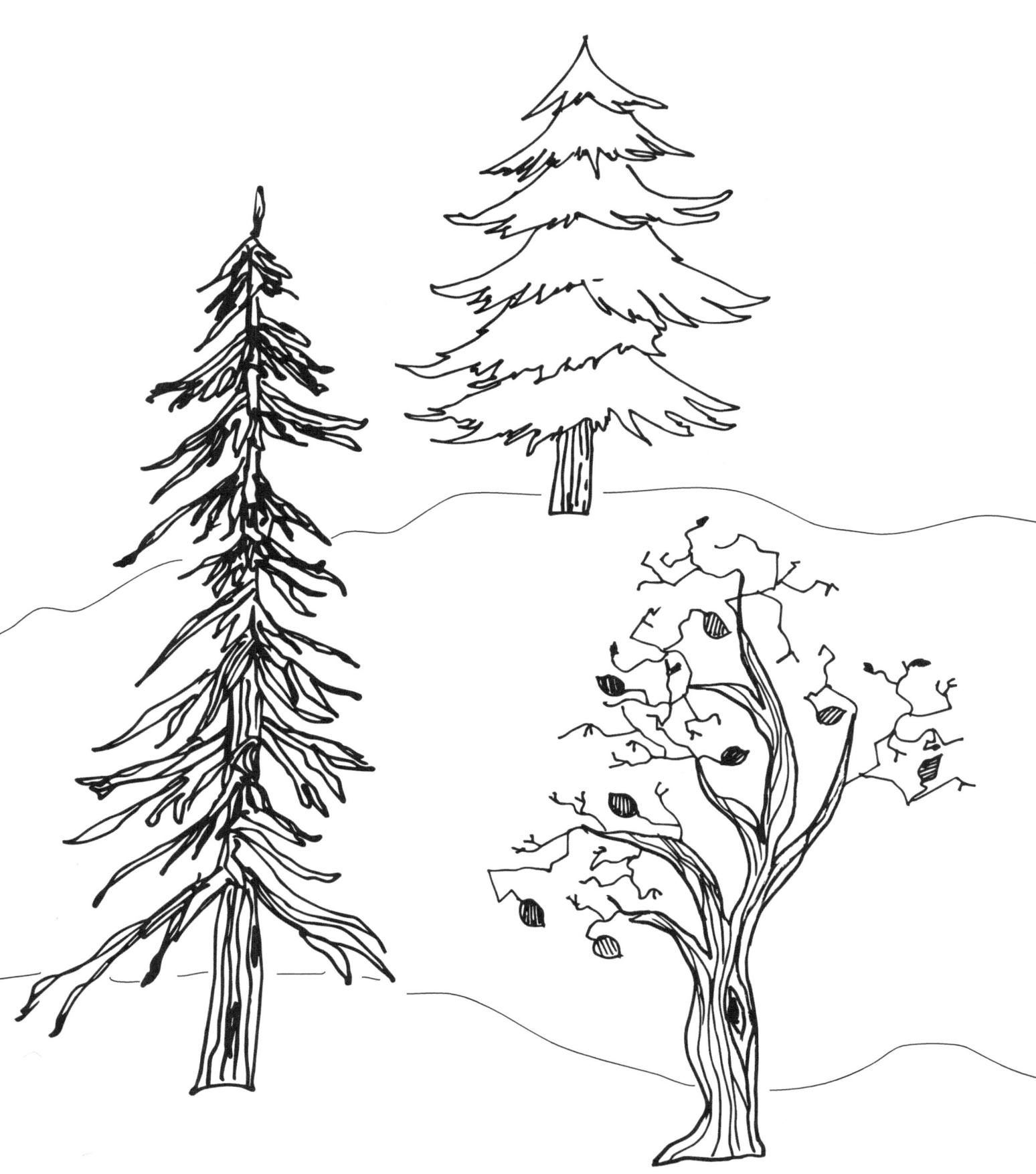

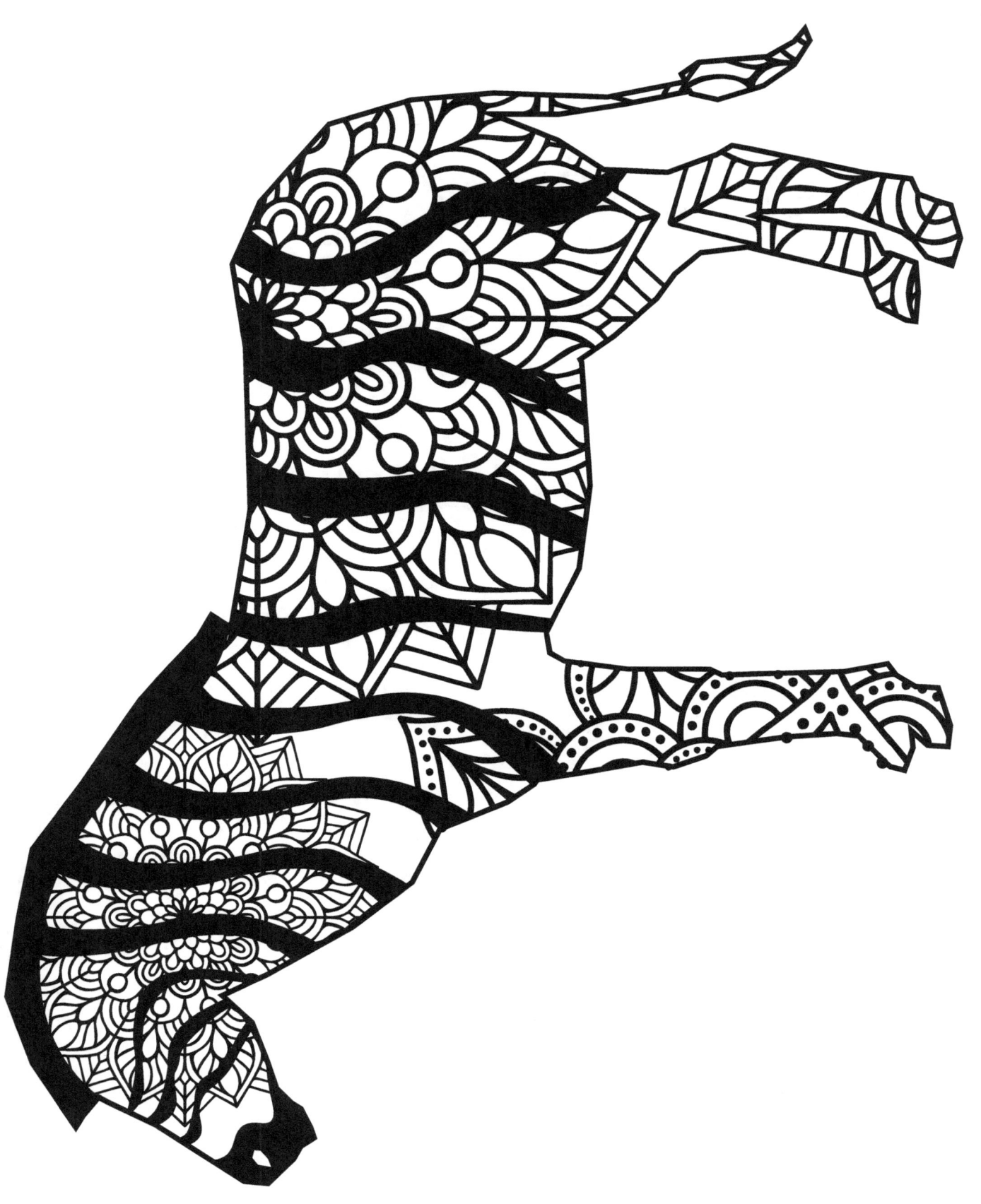

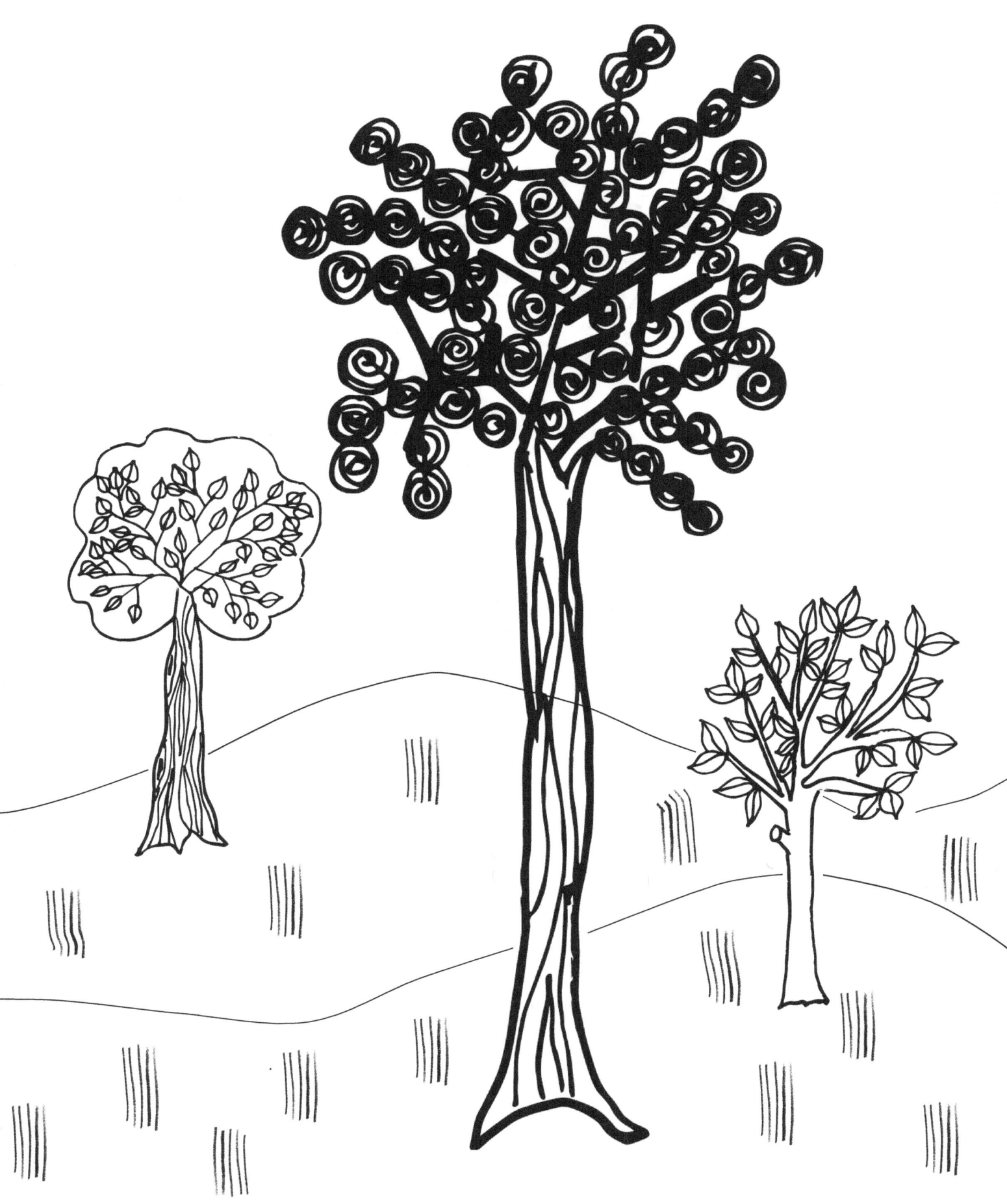

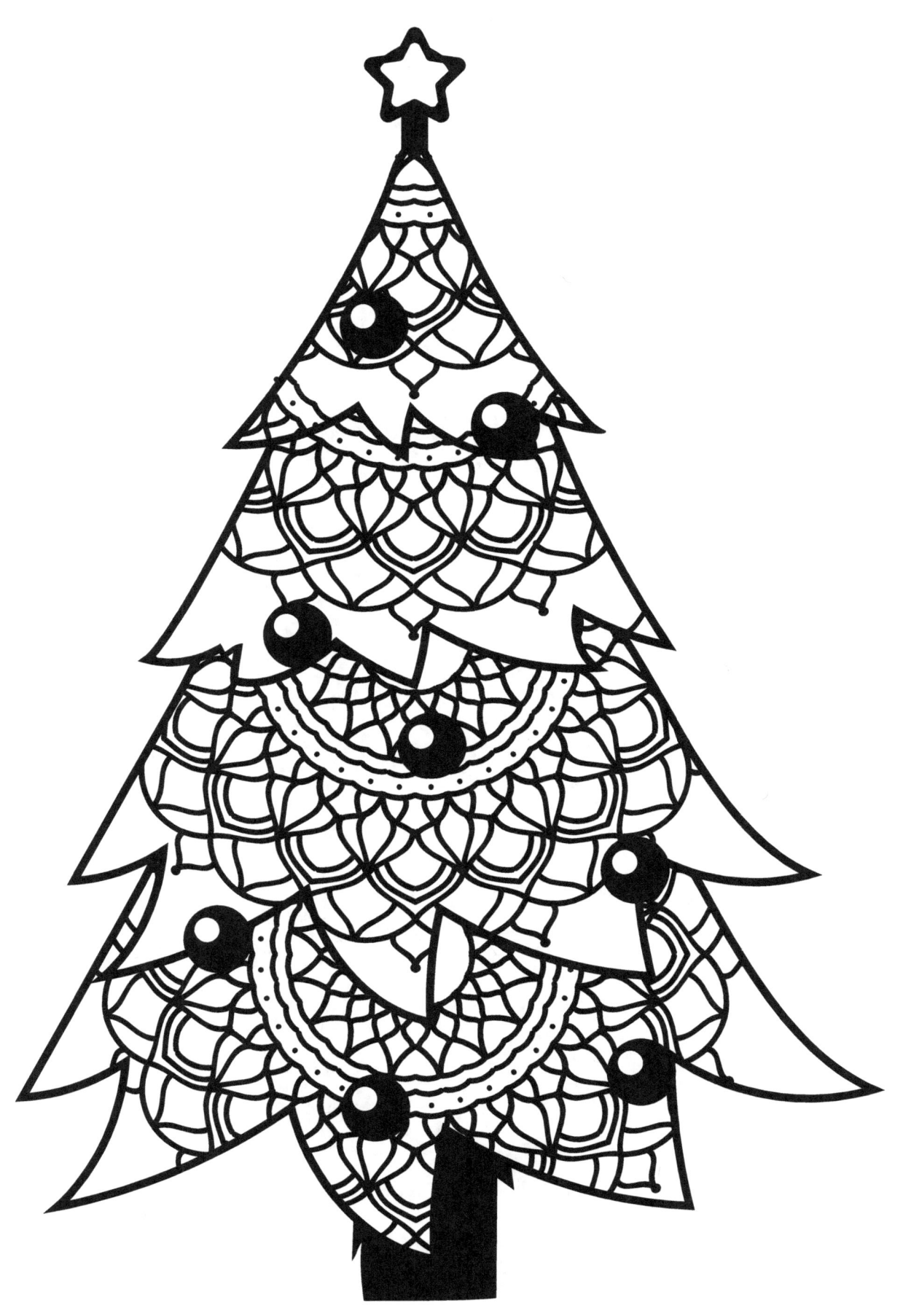

Bonus
Shading and Blending

We've included more complex designs
and a chance for you to show off
your color-blending skills!

Nothing is off limits.
If you want orange grass
and purple clouds, go for it!

If it's realism you want, do that too!

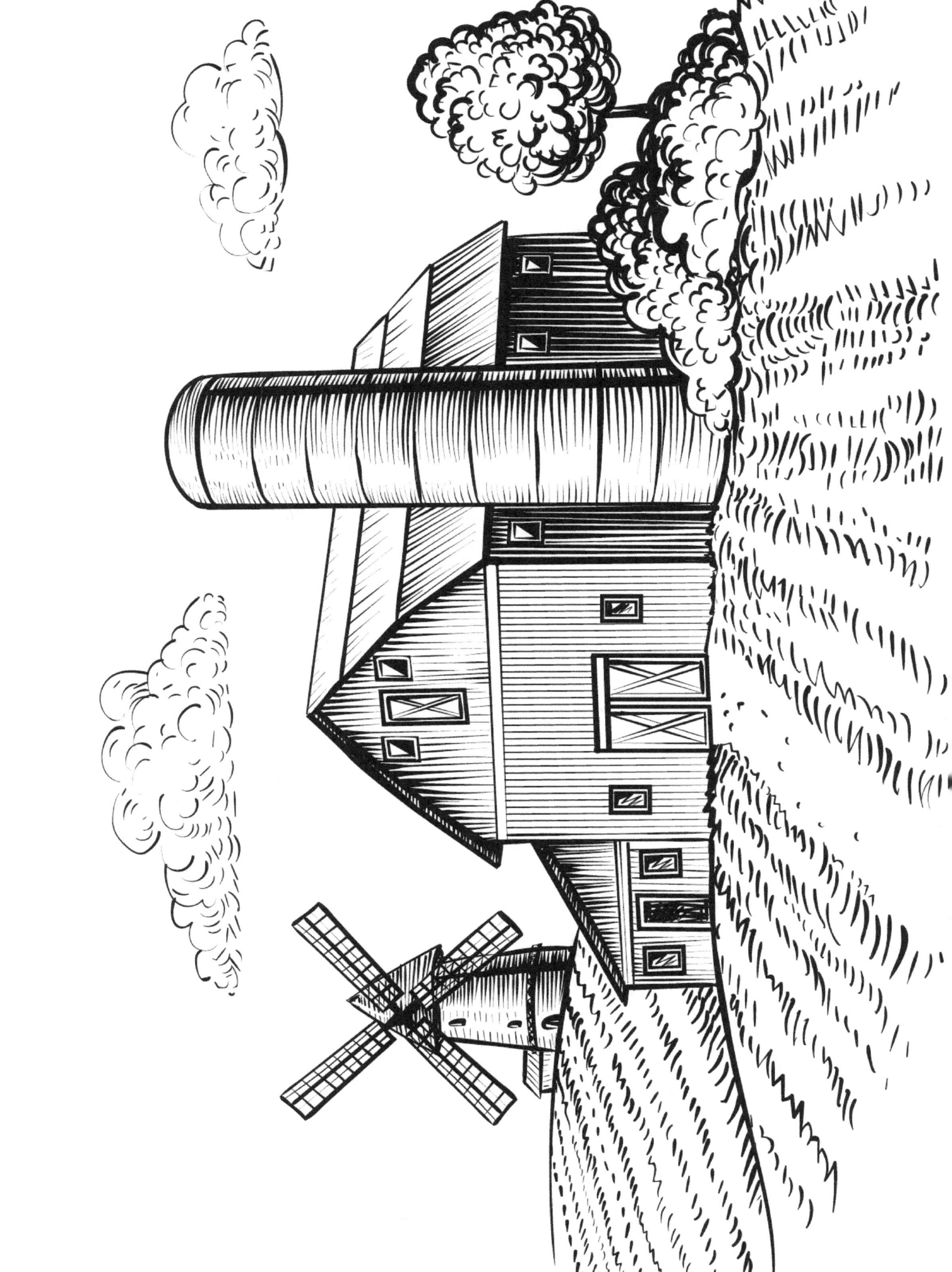

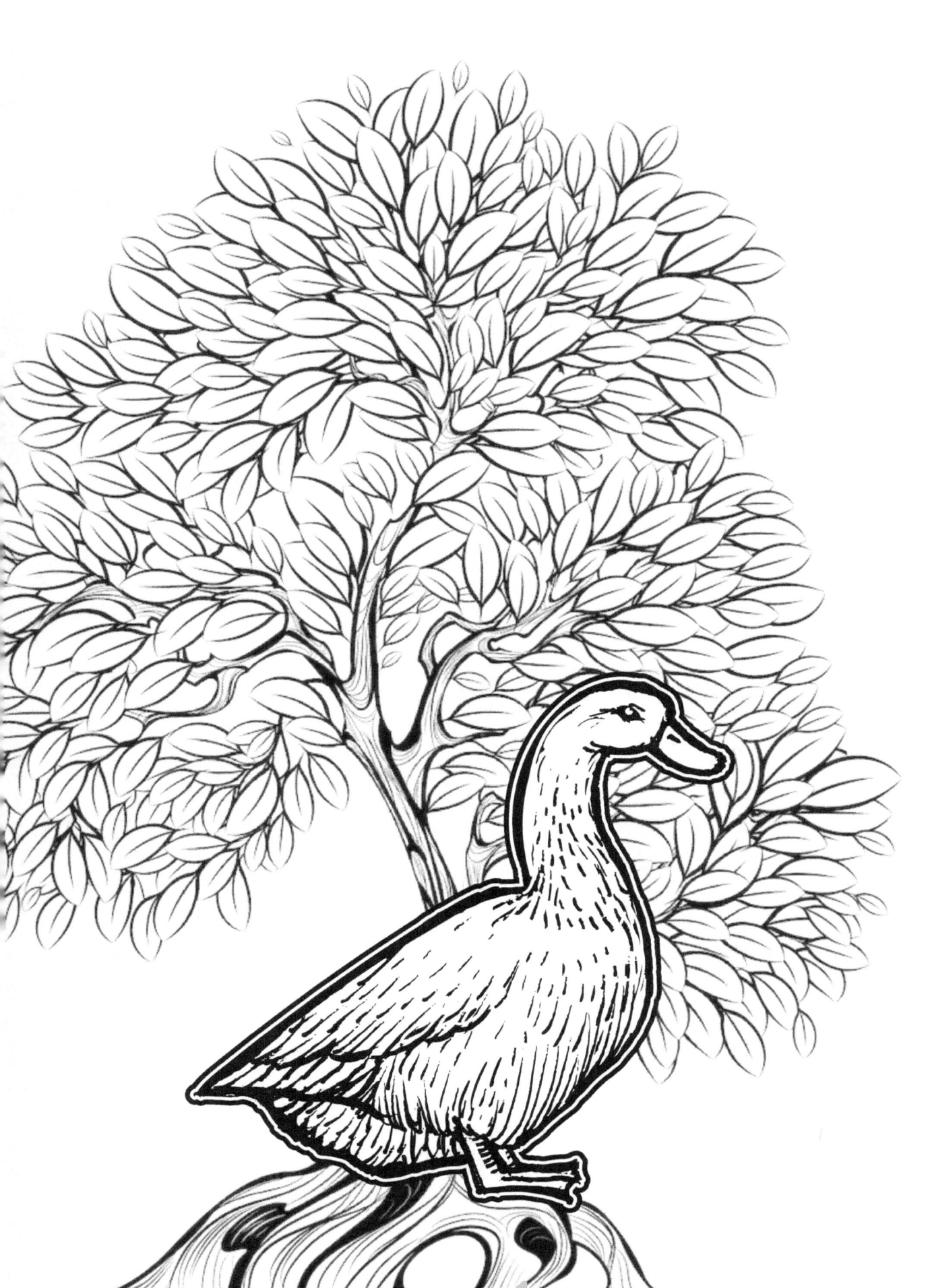

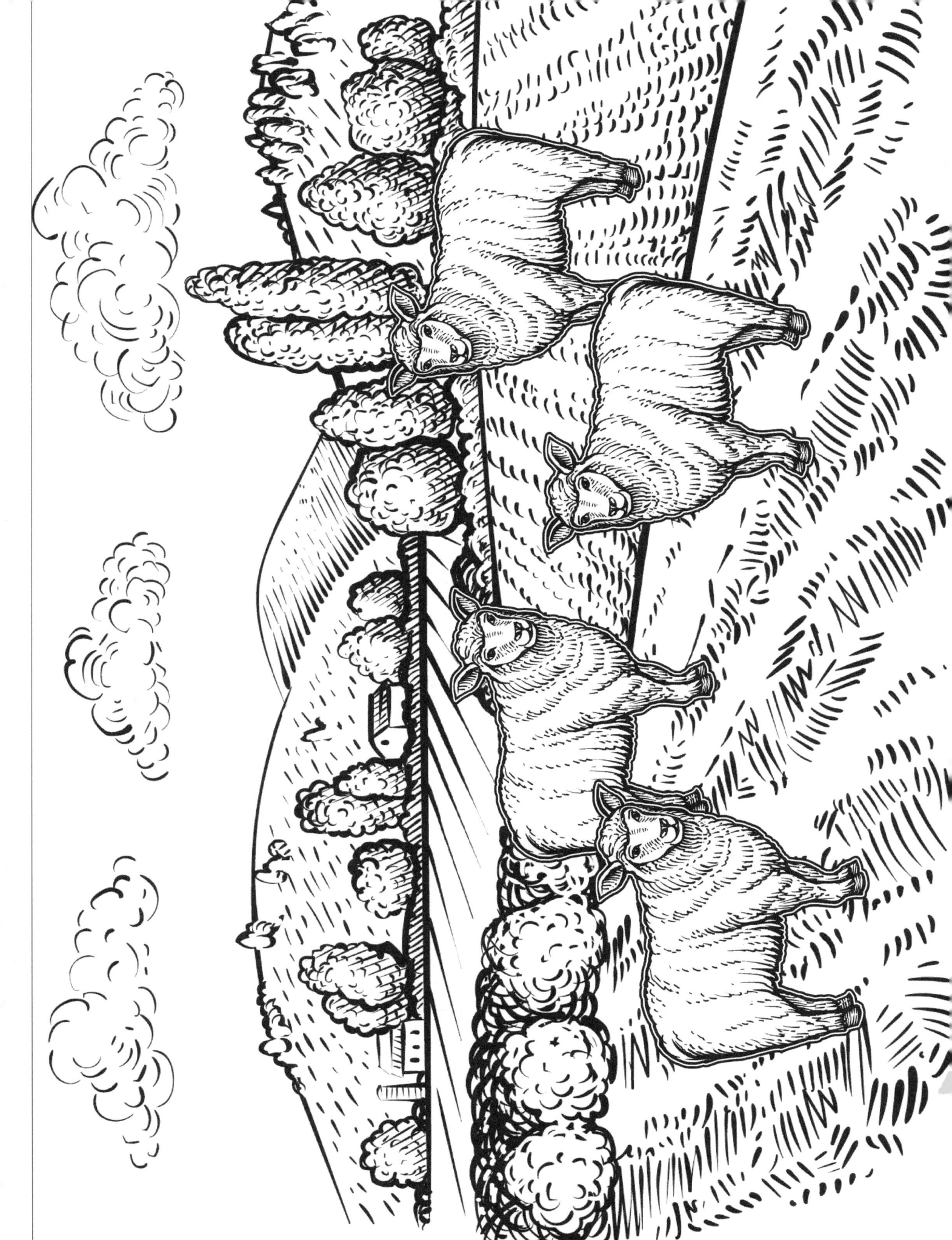

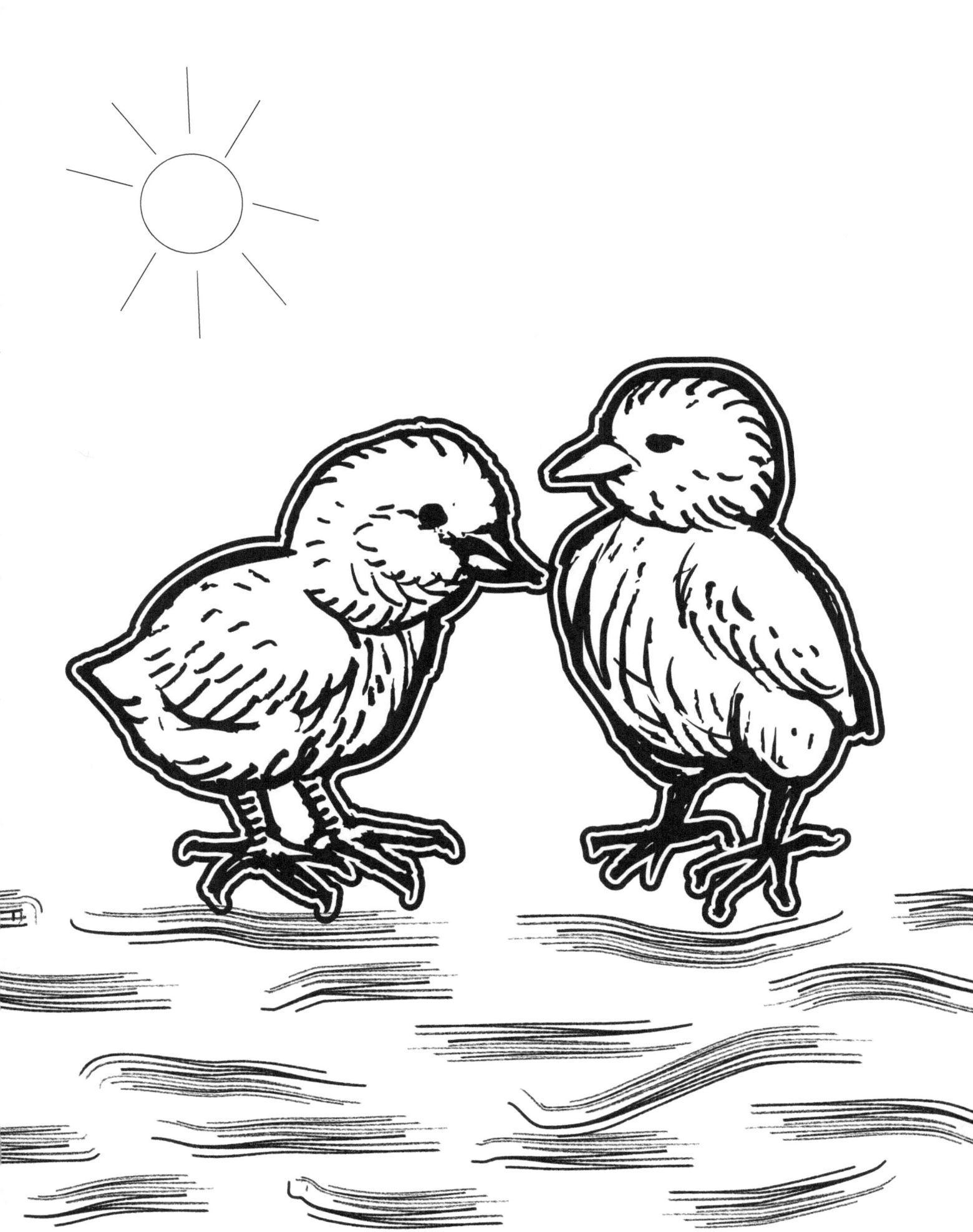

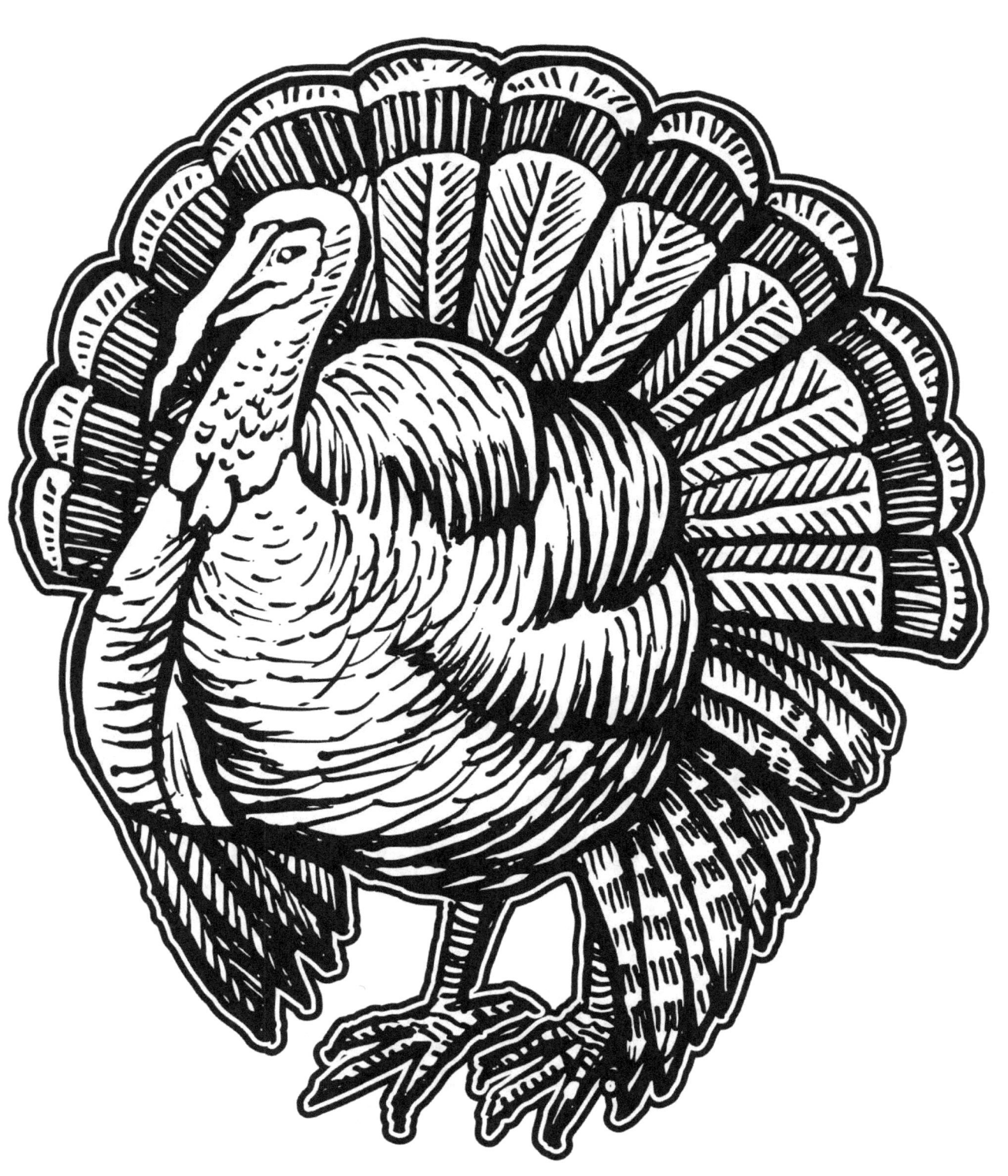

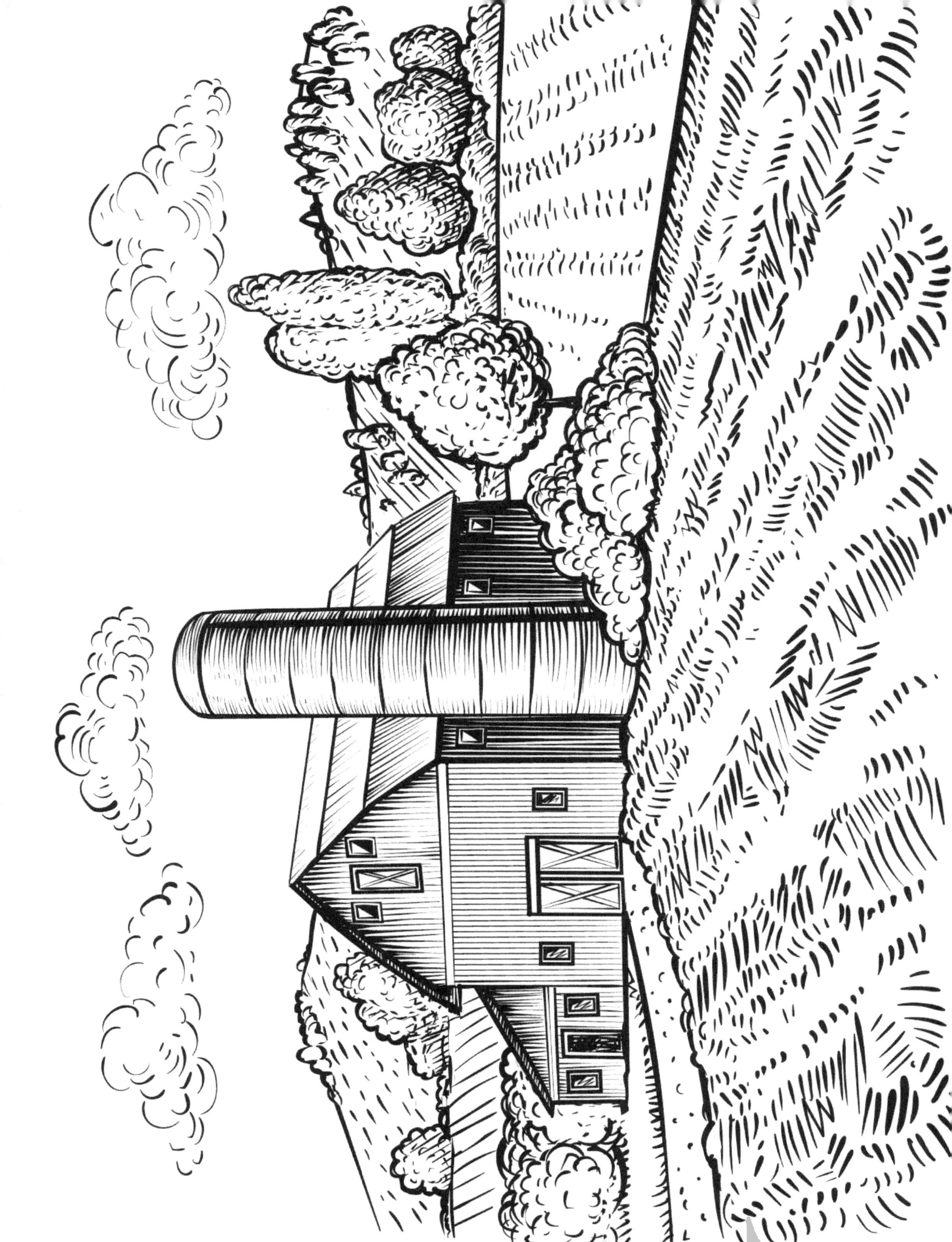

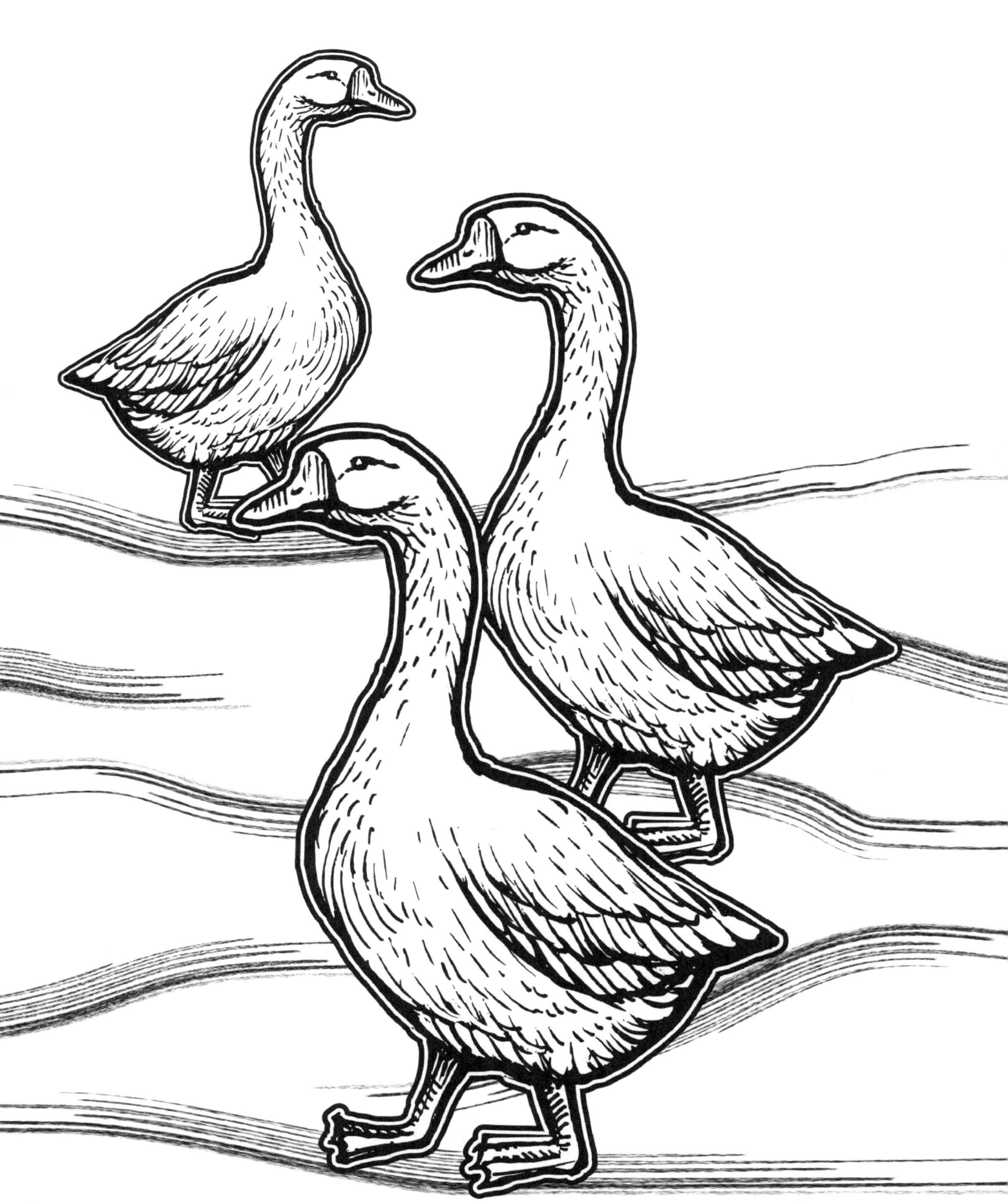

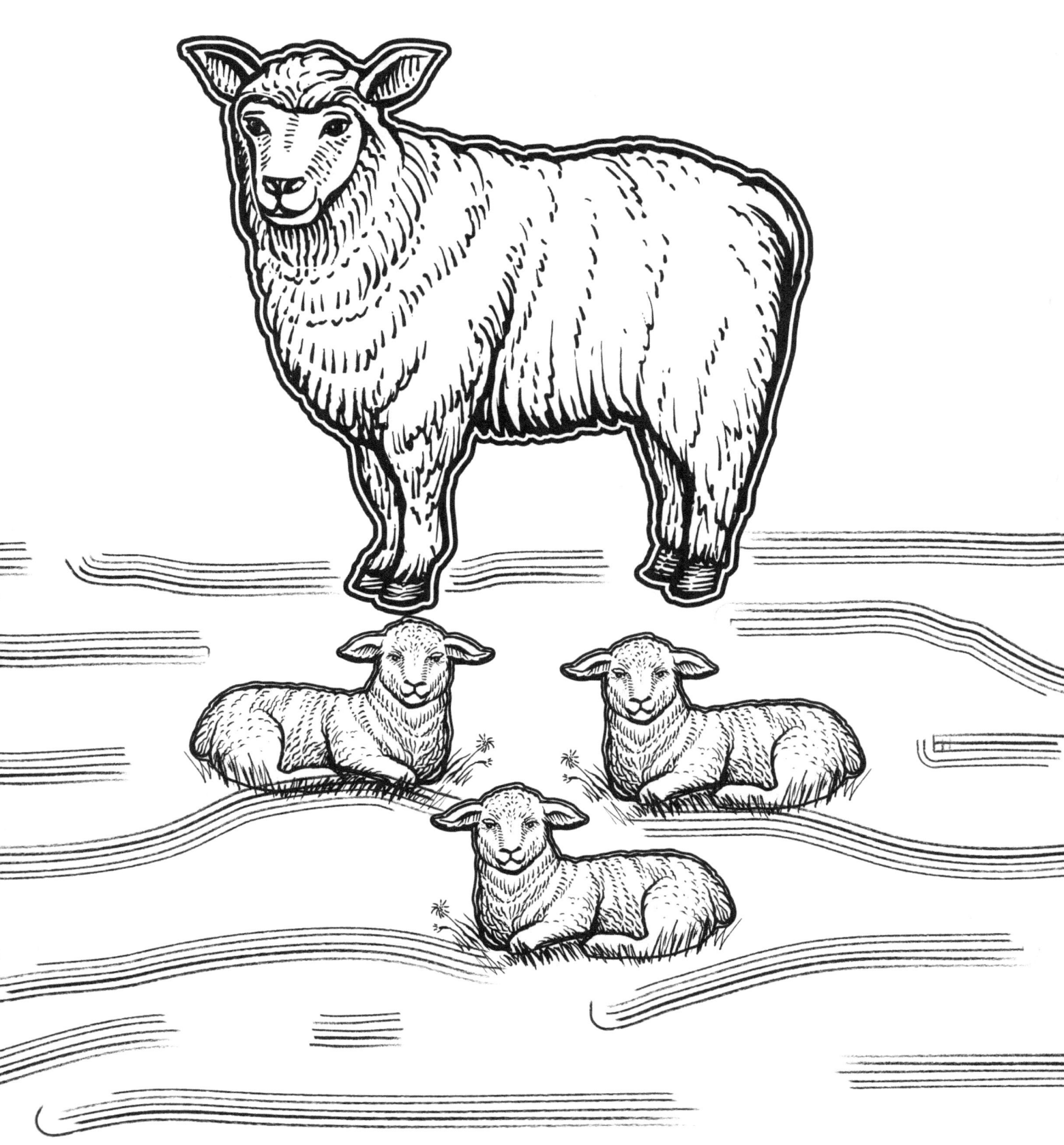

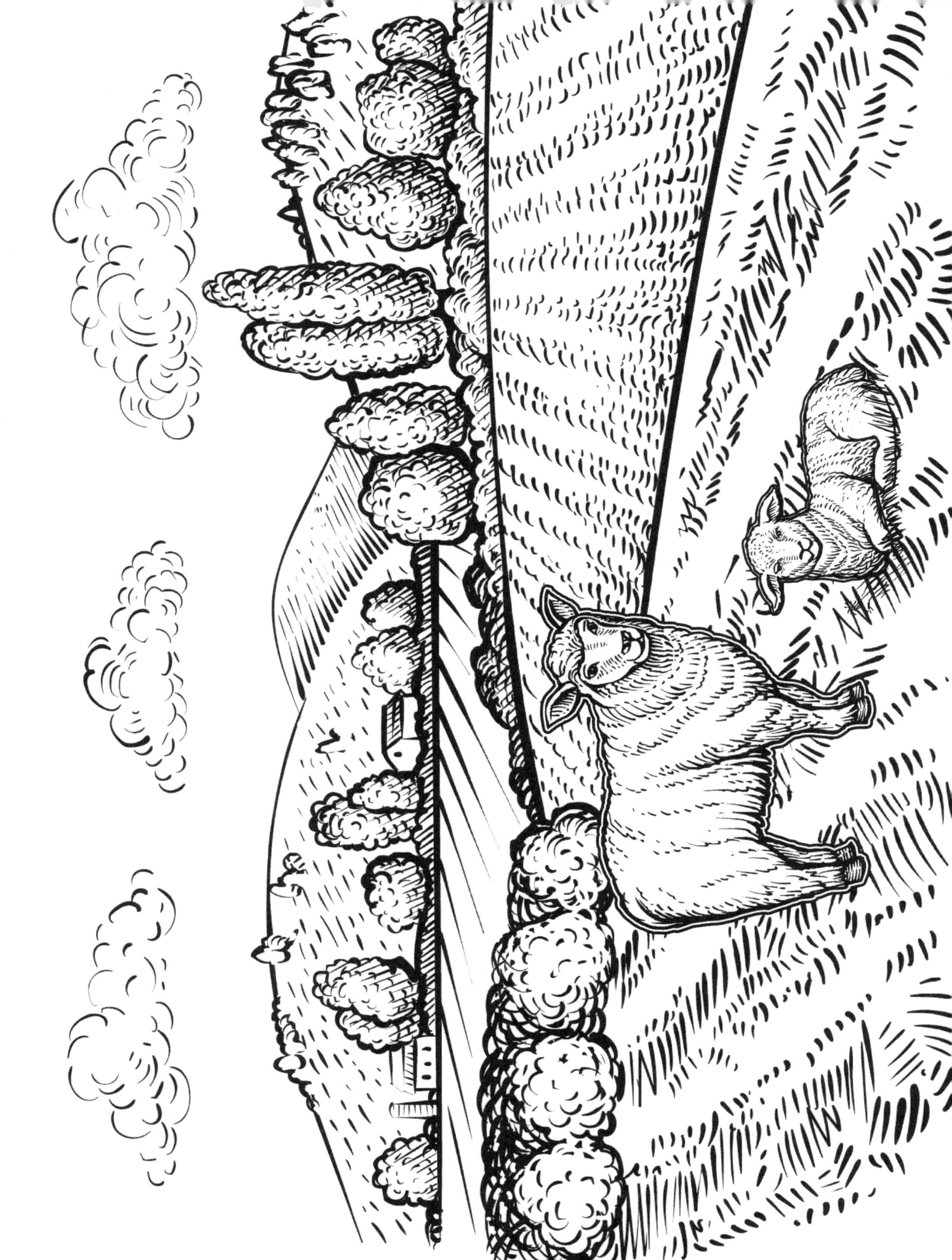

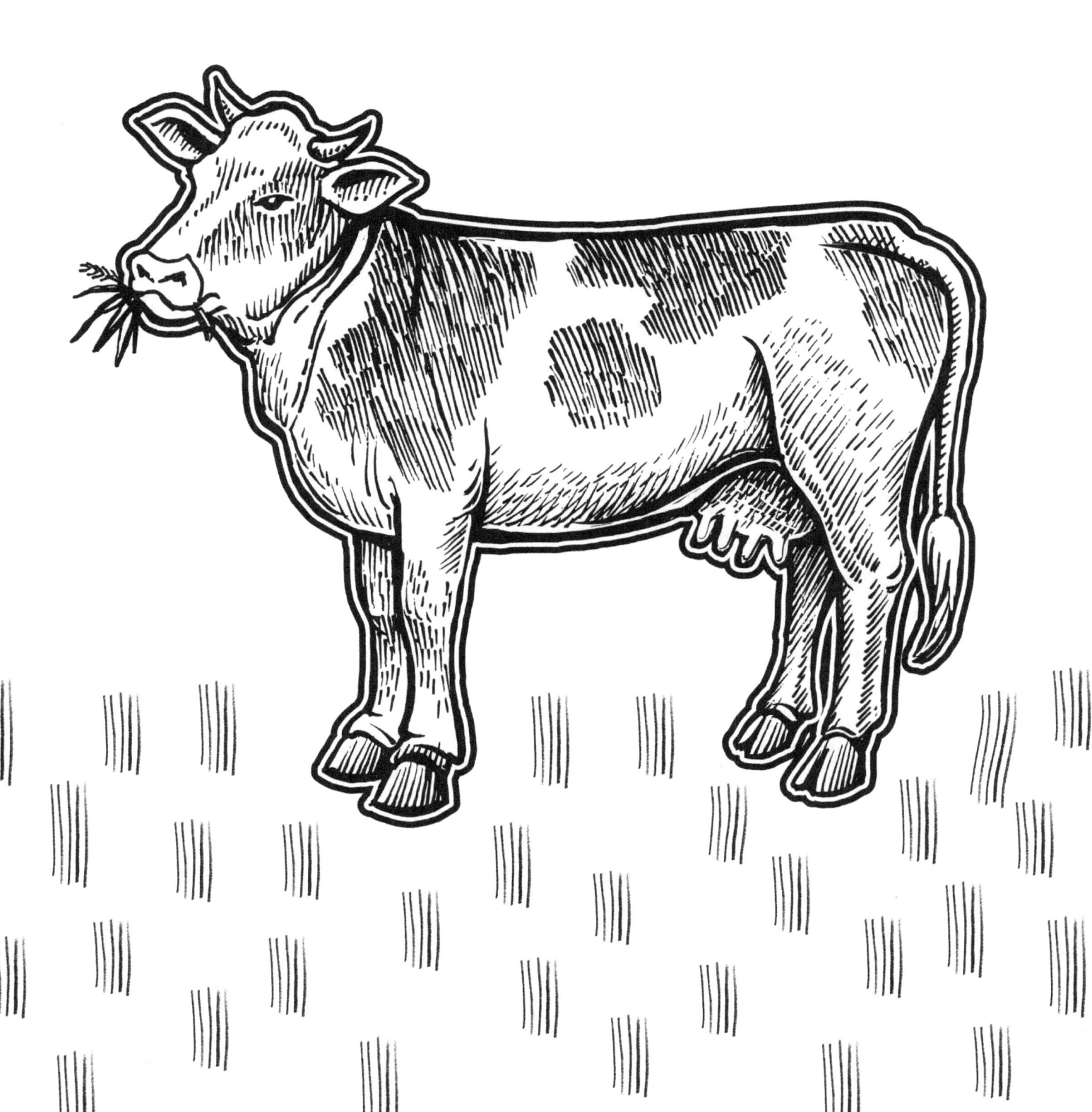

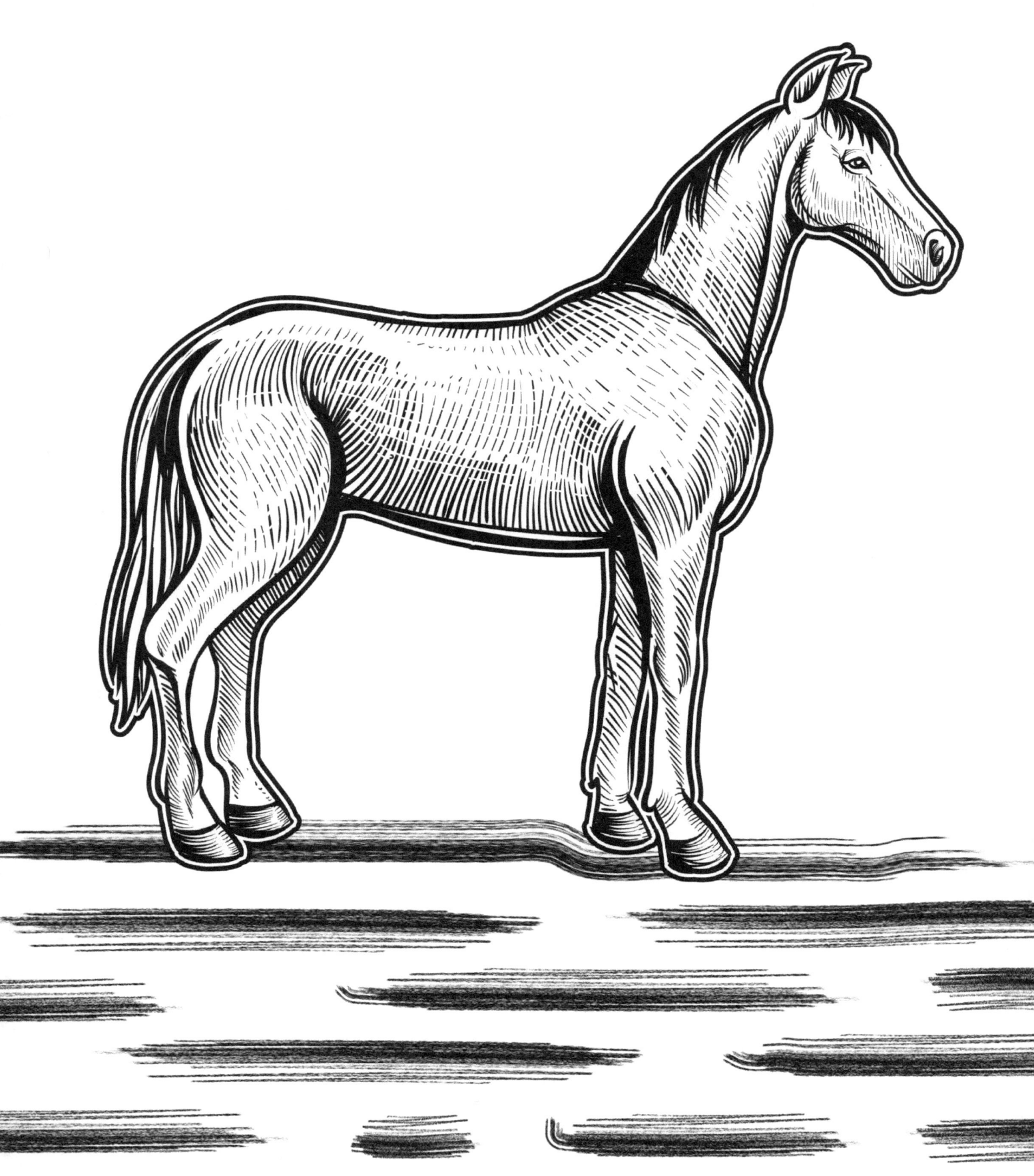

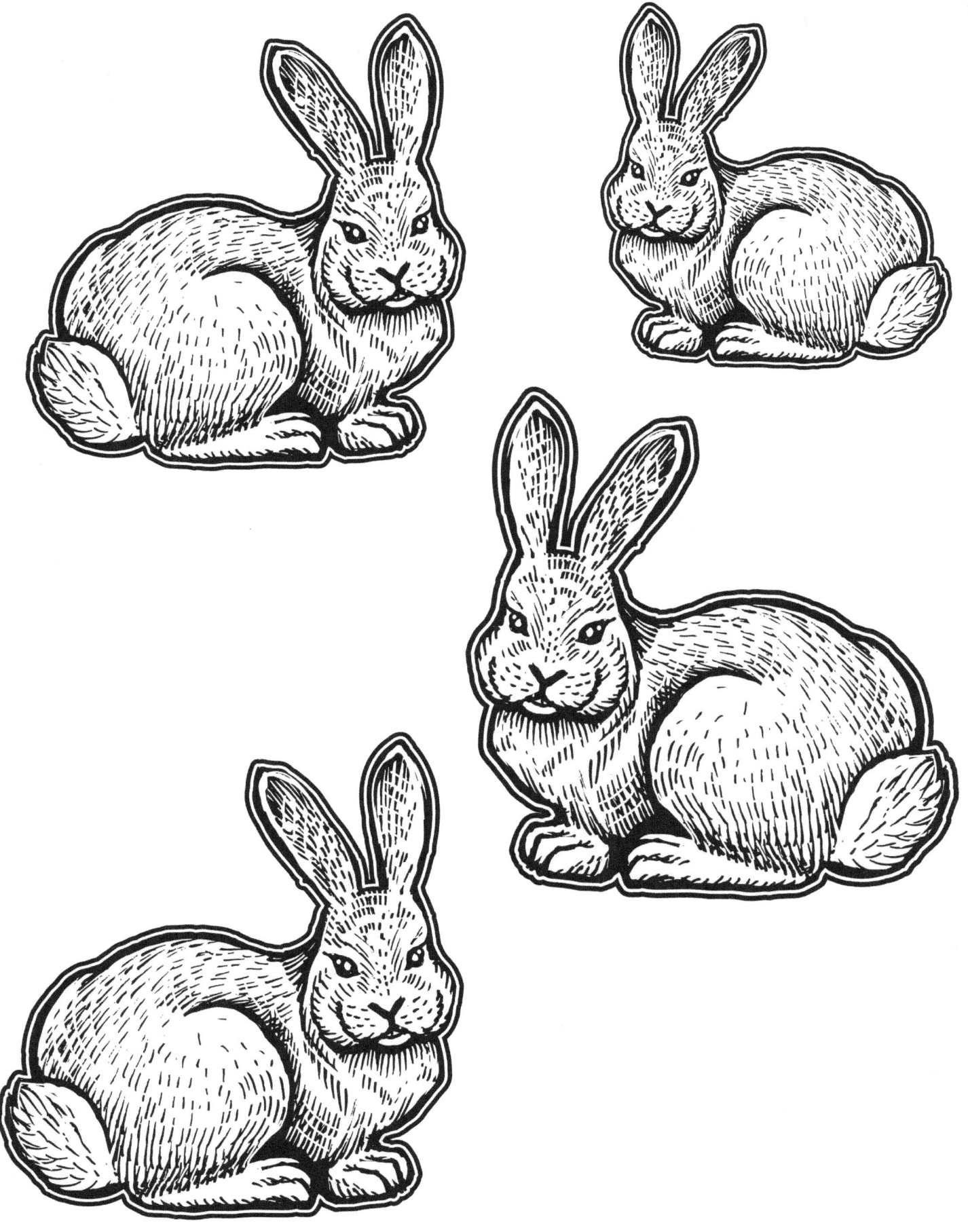

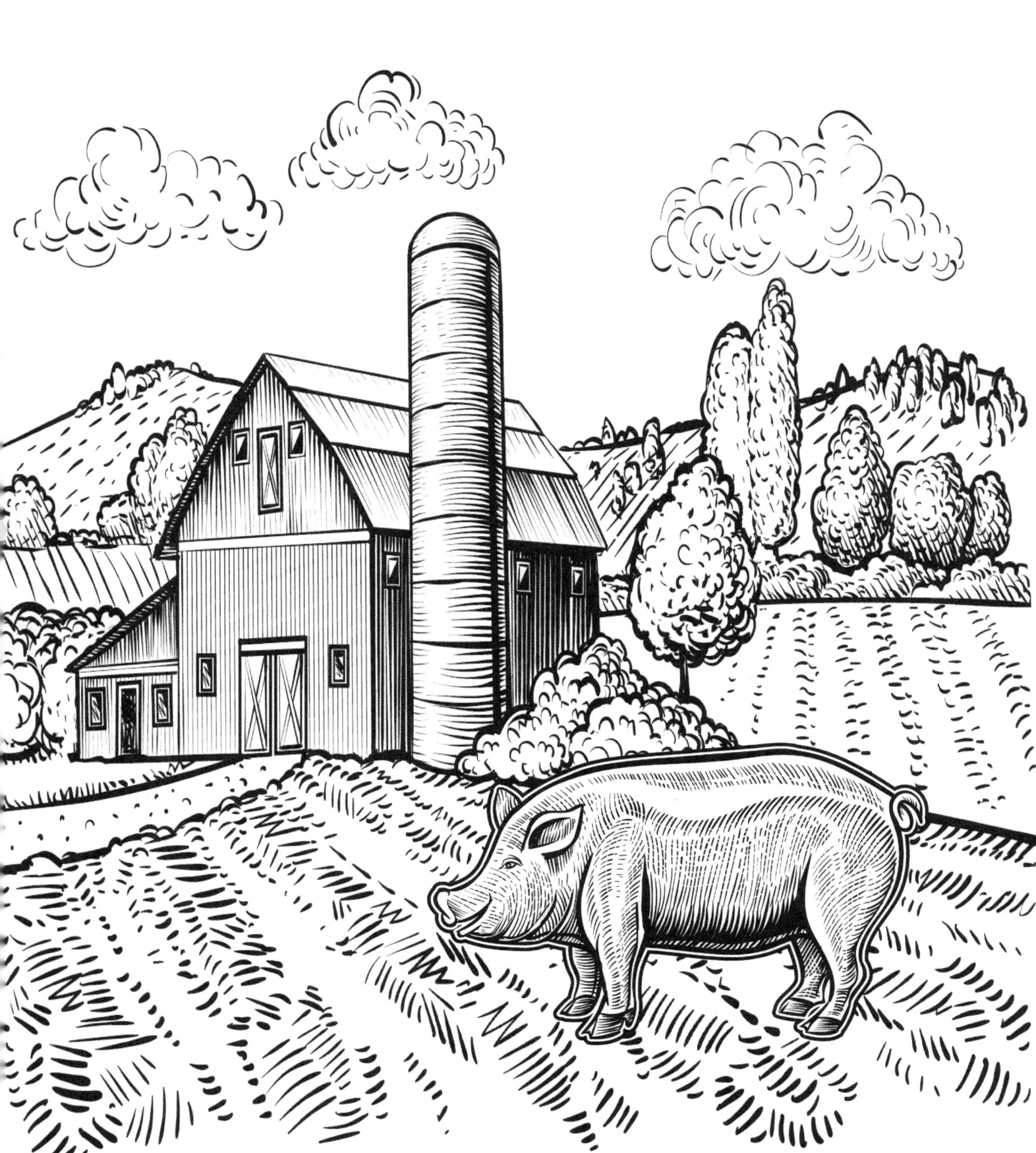

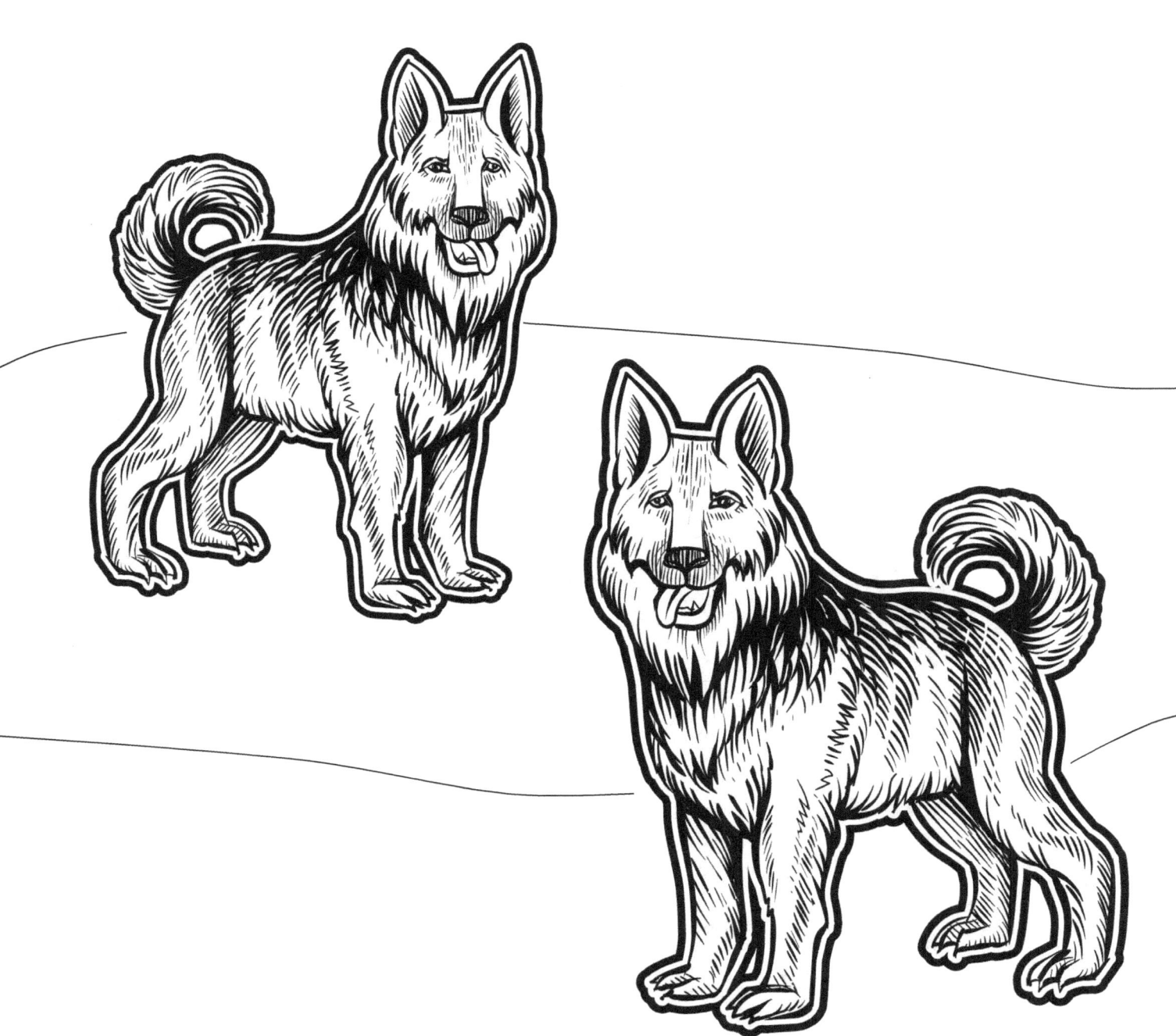

BORED BOOMERS

ADULT COLORING BOOK

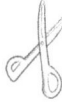

BOOK MARK

I
A M
U P
T O
H E R E

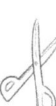

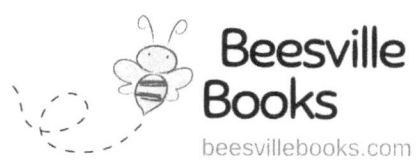

Beesville Books
beesvillebooks.com

Want More?
Drop us a line saying you want more coloring books ~ via our contact page at
BeesvilleBooks.com

We'll add you to our "I want more coloring books" list and our worker bees will let you know FIRST about our new releases!

Bored Boomers want to be in the know. Visit us on Facebook too:
www.facebook.com/BeesvilleBooks

www.ingramcontent.com/pod-product-compliance
Lightning Source LLC
Chambersburg PA
CBHW082025230526
45466CB00023B/3378